FINDING **GOD**
IN YOUR **WORKPLACE**

MON DAY
matters

MARK BILTON

ENDORSEMENTS

"Mark has walked the walk and now he can talk the talk with Monday Matters. When he writes from practical experience it makes the book come to life. Mark goes beyond the idea of just paying bills to get by, or giving God two hours on Sunday and do what you like during the week. The Christian business walk is more than that type of thinking. Read, be challenged but also be encouraged to go for it, which Mark unfolds as God's plan for you."

PETER IRVINE, CO FOUNDER GLORIA JEAN'S COFFEES
AUSTRALIA, SPEAKER AND AUTHOR.

"As Christians, deep inside we know that 'Monday Matters' yet how do we develop spiritual and business disciplines so we can lead integrated lives? Mark Bilton's book "Monday Matters" is about the power of living an integrated Christian life whilst working, Bilton shows us in practical ways how we can delight God through our work. It is an invaluable source of guidance for those who want make their whole lives count seven days a week."

WENDY SIMPSON, CHAIRMAN WENGEO GROUP, AND FORMER
SENIOR VICE PRESIDENT ALCATEL-LUCENT ASIA PACIFIC.

"Work is such a big part of our lives, yet the church has so little to say about it. The rest of the week really does matter to those who passionately seek to live out and express their faith in Jesus 24/7. That's why 'Monday Matters' is such an important and timely book as Mark Bilton helps us discover our godly meaning, purpose and fulfillment through the work that God has anointed for us to do. Definitely one of this year's absolute must-reads."

BERNI DYMET, INTERNATIONAL RADIO PERSONALITY,
AUTHOR, SPEAKER, AND CEO CHRISTIANITY WORKS.

"Mark's book 'Monday Matters' is an absolute must read for every Christian. In a time when there is much debate on the sacred and secular divide; Monday Matters is a refreshing answer to this quandary. I love the simple quote Mark makes about work, 'It is sacred because God ordains it'. This book clearly articulates God's purpose on this earth and mans assignment within the framework of that purpose. I highly recommend this book as every chapter is filled with revelation. I enjoyed every page and can't wait to read more of Mark's writings!"

AMANDA WELLS, BUSINESS OWNER AND PASTOR, PRINCIPAL AND OWNER OF PASSION2PRODUCT COACHING.

"I've had the privilege of meeting Mark Bilton and seeing firsthand his passion for God and love of business. In Monday Matters he clearly and forcefully articulates the high and holy calling of business and, from his own personal experience and the Word, outlines very practical ways of impacting people for Christ in the marketplace. This is no theoretical book but an expression of the heart of a man who lives it."

MICHAEL BAER, CHIEF PEOPLE OFFICER AT EMPLOYBRIDGE USA, INTERNATIONAL SPEAKER AND AUTHOR OF 'BUSINESS AS MISSION'.

"Mark Bilton has put together a tremendous resource in Monday Matters. Mark's relevance as a minister in the marketplace and to others is part of an accelerated convergence taking place because of simple faith and obedience. Join the throng of men an women everywhere who are hearing God's voice in this hour and respond accordingly."

PATRICK MCBANE, FOUNDER AND PRESIDENT OF MARKETPLACE SOLUTIONS, INC.

calledtobusiness.com
finding God at work

Called to Business Press
45 Lawson Parade,
St Ives NSW 2075 AUSTRALIA
Telephone +61 2 99880956
www.CalledtoBusiness.com

Cataloguing in Publication Data:
Title: MONDAY Matters. Finding God in your workplace / Mark Bilton
ISBN: 9780987339805 (paperback)
ISBN: 9780987339812 (ebook)
Subjects: Religion and Theology, Business and Economic
Dewey Number: 248.4

Title Logo by Siah Design
Interior design by Justine Elliott - Book Layout Guru
Images © Olly – Fotolia.com

"I have not stopped giving thanks for you, remembering you in my prayers. I keep asking that the God of our Lord Jesus Christ, the glorious Father, may give you the Spirit of wisdom and revelation, so that you may know him better. I pray that the eyes of your heart may be enlightened in order that you may know the hope to which he has called you, the riches of his glorious inheritance in his holy people, and his incomparably great power for us who believe"

(EPH 1:16–19).

CONTENTS

ACKNOWLEDGMENTS

We all have people in our lives who drive us forward. Some cajole, others encourage, and still others insist we become all we can be. I am blessed with many such people who have nagged, encouraged, prayed, insisted, and persisted to ensure this book was written.

To Ian and Ken, who I meet and pray with regularly, thanks for your teaching and encouragement and those great, deep, but rather early Friday-morning discussions.

To Wendy and Byron, thanks for always insisting on excellence and for your example of living out what you believe in business.

To my loving and ever-patient wife, Helen, a minister to hundreds in her own right, you are my greatest blessing after Christ Himself.

And to my Lord and Savior Jesus, the Hound of Heaven who lovingly and persistently pursued me into the kingdom and literally saved my life, I am and always will be eternally grateful.

INTRODUCTION

There is a move of God happening all around the world. Its expression is diverse and varied, and it is being orchestrated by the Holy Spirit Himself. It seems to have little structure, with no organized leadership, yet it is impacting people, communities, and nations all over the globe.

"I believe one of the next great moves of God is going to be through the believers in the workplace."

—Billy Graham[1]

The move is one borne out of a frustration with an ineffective model that has closeted and constrained Christians to expressing their faith almost exclusively on Sundays. We have segmented and separated our faith into the religious guise of 'sacred.' We have deemed everything else in life to be secular and ensured that the two are distinctly partitioned. The separation of secular and sacred has rendered us ineffective in reaching those around us and impacting our communities.

The concept that God is vitally, passionately, and intimately interested in our workplace, our business, or our place of employment and industry is completely foreign to most of us. However, people have become more aware of the need for change and have embraced the biblical concept of our whole life being impacted by God in recent years. The Marketplace Ministry Movement and Business as Mission are two expressions of an awakening that is occurring across Christendom.

This book has been written to those who want to see God move in their workplaces, whether they are employers or employees. It seeks to understand and illustrate the areas in our work that can be impacted by our relationship with God. It seeks to answer the

---

1   *Faith@Work Movement*, Os Hillman, 2004, Aslan Publishing Group.

simple yet profound question: "How do I integrate my faith into my work?

I am neither an educator nor a theologian. I am first and foremost a follower of Jesus who God has called into the business world. The thoughts, concepts, contentions, and ideas in this book are taken from my 25 years of experience in the commercial arena.

I started as a sales assistant in a menswear store, and God has opened many extraordinary doors that have allowed me to become a managing director and CEO in private, public, and multinational companies. The companies I have led were in diverse industries, and they often had significant challenges and needed comprehensive change.

I am still learning and still growing, and God still has me in the commercial world. It is where I am most effective because He has equipped and gifted me to serve Him in this area. There have been down times as well as good times, but throughout it all, God has proved to be faithful, true, and an ever-present help. God took me as a disillusioned, depressed, and struggling 20-year-old and revolutionized my life. The lessons I have learned and their application in the workplace are all here in this book.

My desire is to see businesspeople all over the world be released into the freedom and knowledge of God's plan and purpose in the workplace. With revelation and empowerment, potential is released and dreams are realized. God has a plan and a purpose for your life, and it has been my experience that, without exception, we are all anointed and appointed for a specific purpose.

CHAPTER 1
WHY WORK?

"The Lord God took the man and put him in the Garden of Eden to work it and take care of it"

(GEN 2:15).

Work. What do you think of when you hear that word? It is usually associated with something that is hard. Perhaps your work life is boring, mundane, and mindless. For others it is stressful, challenging, and soul sapping. For most of us it is a way of earning a living, paying the bills, and providing for our families. Work is often just endured or thought of as a necessary evil.

Our culture says, "Let's work so we can enjoy the weekend," and "Thank God it is Friday." But what about Monday? It is often greeted with a gritting of teeth and a dread of the never-ending cycle of getting up, going to work, and coming home. Surely there must be something more to life than this!

What about the Christian worldview? We are saved, and God has a plan and purpose for our lives. Most of us acknowledge that, even if it is only intellectually. Yet there is within many of us an innate misunderstanding that God is only really interested in what we do spiritually. Perhaps for pastors, priests, or missionaries God may be interested in what they do during the week, but they are, after all, set apart for God's work—right?

This is a very prevalent perception in our Western Christian worldview, yet it is entirely and totally unscriptural. It is a delusion that has rendered most of the laity—the everyday, normal churchgoing person, the worker—impotent and unaware of God's mandate and purpose for our lives.

There is another way, a way that is rewarding, purposeful, satisfying and ordained by God. My Bible tells me in Colossians 3:23, *"Whatever may be your task, work at it heartily (from the soul), as [something done] for the Lord and not for men"* (AMP).

The key word in this Scripture is *whatever*. Does whatever include what I do on a Sunday in church? Yes, it does. Does it also refer to whatever I do during my week at work? Definitely and absolutely, yes it does. If that is the case, then why don't we talk more about how we can integrate our faith into our work? What does working for the Lord while we are at work look like?

The secular-sacred divide

We have made a significant error in our postmodern society when we have separated what is sacred from what is secular. There should be no separation between the secular and the sacred. This is an artificial construct we have adopted almost since the establishment of Christianity as a state religion back in the days of Constantinople. You can work out your God-given gifts, talents, and calling in a business role just as much as you can while leading a religious institution.

Mark Greene of the London Institute for Contemporary Christianity, in his excellent publication *The Great Divide*, draws an insightful analogy from fruit:

> SSD (Sacred Secular Divide) is the pervasive belief that life is an orange not a peach, that some segments of our life are really important to God—prayer, church services, church-based activities - but that others aren't— work, school, university, sport, the arts, music, rest, sleep, hobbies. SSD is like a virus. It pervades the church and pretty much everyone I know has it and is a carrier. I've had it. And I struggle against it all the time.[2]

This unfortunate manmade perspective is perpetuating an abstract spirituality, which bears little resemblance to a complete whole life theology. It also has the consequence of limiting God and His impact to those activities we have labeled sacred.

However, according to Colossians 1:20, God wants *"to reconcile to himself all things, whether things on earth or things in heaven, by making peace through his blood, shed on the cross."*

Your place in the world

God has made you unique. You are one of a kind. There is no other person like you, and there never will be. God has created

---

2 *The Great Divide*, Mark Greene. Online: http://www.intheworkplace. com/apps/articles/default.asp?articleid=12783&columnid=1935.

you specifically and on purpose. He has given you a unique combination of talents and gifts and a certain temperament and personality. You know you are good at some things and not at others. God has imbued you with specific passions and dreams.

Some people are detail orientated, and others just see the big picture. There are some things we will never be good at. It is easy to envy those who have developed the gifts we don't possess, but we are a special blend of all God has made us to be.

Just as we are created uniquely, He also has a unique and specific purpose for us to fulfill. We are told in Scripture that He has a purpose and a plan for our lives—one to prosper us and not to harm us (see Jer 29:11). He has planned out things for us to do—divine appointments, impacts, and good deeds preordained for us to fulfill. The vast majority of us spend almost all our time at work. Would God really have a plan only for the minority of time we spend outside of work? That sounds like a waste to me. We are not called to limit our Christian expressions and experiences to our spare time.

Perhaps you are working and waiting for God to call you into 'ministry.' Some people, quite rightly, are called into fulltime church service, and some are called to go to other countries as missionaries. However, we are all called to the ministry—to work out God's purposes in our everyday lives.

The calling you are waiting for, the mission field you are looking for, and the anointing you are asking for are all available, right here where you are right now. Perhaps God is calling you to stay and fulfill your purpose where you are.

If you are surrendered to God and doing what He is asking you to do, that constitutes a call. If you are called by God, then you are empowered by God. The gifts and fruit of the Spirit we have can manifest just as well when we are in a secular role as when we are fulltime workers in a church environment. God is completely interested in the details of your everyday life and vocation. He can and will use you where you are, whether it is in the marketplace or as a missionary in a foreign land.

We need to challenge our worldview. We have taken our world and separated into the secular and the sacred. Our Christian week and our Christian experience are confined to Sunday, plus maybe a Wednesday night home group, and the holiest of us might make the prayer meeting. Often we judge our dedication, commitment, and spirituality by how much of our spare time is taken up by church activities.

Church leaders are also susceptible to this view and can often perpetuate this perspective. Quite rightly, they are interested primarily in looking after and growing the local church. Let me say categorically and with no hesitation that the local church is a valid and important institution. We should all be committed to a local body of believers and commit ourselves to being a part of that community. *But* there is so much more for us to do and to be as we exercise our ministry in the marketplace as God's believers. We are all priests and kings who have been called by God. We are anointed and appointed for a God-given purpose.

Imagine what it would be like if our church leaders took the view that they were only working for the weekend— that they were just preaching and ministering to pay the mortgage. That sounds ludicrous, doesn't it? We certainly would not be too comfortable sitting under that kind of leadership in a church context. Yet we are quite willing to apply it to our own lives. Why? If God places you in a specific role, surely He has a plan and a purpose for you being there. If there is a purpose, then will He not also equip you accordingly? If God desires for you to be effective, He will equip you just as He would anyone else He calls, whether it be a pastor, priest, missionary, or fulltime church worker.

Often as business leaders or career workers, we denigrate our roles as just providing finances for the kingdom of God. We are funding the 'end times,' if you will. This is an important part, but it is in no way the totality of our call to business.

We are called to serve, to minister, and to witness so we can co-create with God to see His kingdom come into our sphere of influence. We are required to demonstrate the Christian life, to minister to those around us, and to witness to the lost. We are empowered to bring reconciliation to the immediate workplace and the wider marketplace. We have been empowered to serve and to have influence in society for good. If we really got a hold of that truth, we would surely turn the world upside down.

According to Matthew 5, we are called to business to be *"salt and light"*—salt to cleanse and preserve and light to dispel darkness and bring warmth. Jesus left us a very clear mission statement in Mark 16:15: *"Go into all the world and preach the gospel to all creation."*

That means all of us in the entire world. Wherever we find ourselves is our world. It is a big challenge, and what it asks of us is certainly daunting. However, God will never ask us to do anything He will not provide the courage for us to complete. He will provide all we need for everything He asks us to do.

God wonderfully, fully, and completely loves every person. He is no respecter of persons (see Acts 10:35). He views the king and the slave alike. Just as we are all valued equally, the roles we are given are equally important. The Scriptures talk about the body that we are all a part of. Every part has a specific, critical role and purpose. Some are hidden or small but still vital. In fact, it is often the hidden parts that are most important and the obvious parts that are more superficial. We can live without a hand but not without a liver.

What does God think about work?

In our modern Christian culture, we have a heretical hierarchical view of vocations. This is a cultural bias, not a God-given one. We have created an artificial construct of levels of service, topped by pastors, missionaries, and 'fulltime' workers for God, followed by workers of service, nurses, teachers, social workers, and others. We then descend into the depths of the mundane and the ungodly that the rest of us occupy. At the bottom are the accountants, lawyers, and merchant bankers. I jest, but you get the point. This worldview is a deception that is diametrically opposed to the truth. In my view, it is intended to contain the impact of God that would undoubtedly result if we really understood the meaning of being called for a purpose in the marketplace, day-by-day, hour-by-hour and minute-by-minute.

Even the word vocation comes from the root verb, 'to call' the same one that we get the word 'vocal' from. Vocation literally means a calling, something specifically ordained by God. We have each been assigned a place.

"Each one should retain the place in life that the Lord assigned to him and to which God has called him" (1 COR 7:17 NIV1984).

We are called to be all we can be regardless of the role we are assigned to. Martin Luther wrote, *"A cobbler, a smith, a farmer, by means of his own work or office must benefit and serve every other, that in this way many kinds of work may be done for the bodily and spiritual welfare of the community, even as all the members of the body serve one another."*[3]

We are called to stay more often than to go. Doing what you do is the basis of your service to God. He will use you where you are, change you where you are, and grow you where you are. We need to learn to see the sacred in the seemingly ordinary to appreciate God's plan for our lives.

As we submit to God in this, the motivation will come, the fruit of the Spirit will be manifested, and true ministry will begin to occur. God has given us authority over all things. Even in the beginning, God blessed Adam and Eve and said to them in Genesis

---

3 *Address to the Christian Nobles of the German Nation,* Martin Luther, 1520.

1:28, *"Be fruitful and increase in number; fill the earth and subdue it. Rule over the fish in the sea and the birds in the sky and over every living creature that moves on the ground."*

God called us to work from the very beginning. Our work's intrinsic value is not determined by whether it happens in a secular or sacred environment. It is sacred because God ordains it. He values a call to business just as much as any other call. It is a sacred vocation that is made sacred because God mandates it. He uses it to fulfill His purpose in our lives and calls us to serve in a way that is in line with His way: virtuous, ethical, and with excellence, *"as if serving the Lord."*

It is often stated that God demonstrated the Sabbath by resting on the seventh day. As it says in Genesis 2:2, *"By the seventh day God had finished the work he had been doing; so on the seventh day he rested from all his work."* This is very valid and clearly demonstrated a way of honoring God and refreshing ourselves for the next week of labor, but God also demonstrated what it was to work on the other six days. The week was staged, managed, checked, assessed, and found to be good. One day laid a foundation for the next, and there was progression, planning, strategy, execution, contemplation, and evaluation. As Genesis 1:31 says, *"God saw all that he had made, and it was very good."*

We may all have heard the saying from Luke 12:7, *"Indeed, the very hairs of your head are all numbered."* It has to be said that some heads are easier to count than others. That aside, it does demonstrate God is interested in the detail—in the smallest part of His creation. Any close inspection of the details in any insect, flower, or any part of His wonderful creation will testify to that. If it is true that every hair is numbered and as Psalm 139:16 tells us, *"All the days ordained for me were written in your book before one of them came to be,"* then surely every small part of every day was accounted for. We have no days off from working out His purposes in us, through us, for us, and for those around us. He didn't forget Monday to Friday. It is not all about Sunday, which is when we get refreshed and equipped to go out again and work out our faith in the real world.

God has a very real job for you to do. It includes your employment or business and can be rewarding and full of purpose. God created work. The very concept was birthed in Him. The Bible is full of references to work, even in the beginning, in Genesis. Work was God's idea.

"The Lord God took the man and put Him in the Garden of Eden to work it and take care of it" (GEN 2:15).

Work came before the fall as Adam and Eve worked in the garden. They were given things to do. They had to tend the garden, name the animals, take authority, and work with the resources they had. This was at a time when sin had not yet entered the world.

The garden of Eden is the clearest view we have of a perfect world, of eternity, or of what heaven may be like. It was a world without blemish or sin. If you think heaven is sitting around on a cloud playing a harp, then that is another worldview that needs to shift. How boring would that be? When the curse came, it was the ground that was cursed, not work.

"To Adam he said, 'Because you listened to your wife and ate from the tree about which I commanded you, "You must not eat of it," Cursed is the ground because of you; through painful toil you will eat of it all the days of your life'" (GEN 3:17).

There is a distinct and very important distinction to make here. Our work is not a result of sin or of our fallen state. The ground has been cursed as a consequence sin's entry into the world, so yes, there will be toil because we live in a fallen world; there are always consequences for sin. But God sent the second Adam, Jesus, to redeem us from the curse. Work in its sanctified state is intrinsically good and deemed important by God. Indeed, work is ordained by God.

There is an understanding in scriptural study called the 'law of first-mention.' It is the principle in the interpretation of Scripture, that states that the first mention or occurrence of a biblical subject establishes an unchangeable pattern, with that subject remaining unchanged in the mind of God throughout Scripture. The initial mention is the most significant, and it sets the pattern for the understanding of the principle.

Are you ready for this, because when I first heard this, I just about fell over? It was a great comfort and certainly confirmed my views. For whom did God reserve the first recorded infilling of the Holy Spirit? A king? A priest? A prophet? No, it was an ordinary guy named Bezalel. He was a craftsman, a worker, and a builder. Read the account for yourself.

"Then Moses said to the Israelites, 'See, the Lord has chosen Bezalel son of Uri, the son of Hur, of the tribe of Judah, **and He has filled him with the Spirit of God,** *with wisdom, with understanding, with knowledge and with all kinds of skills—to make artistic designs for work in gold, silver and bronze, to cut and set stones, to work in wood and to engage in all kinds of artistic crafts. And He has given both him and Oholiab son of Ahisamak, of the tribe of Dan, the ability to teach others. He has filled them with skill to do all kinds of work as engravers, designers, embroiderers in blue, purple and scarlet yarn and fine linen, and weavers, all of them skilled workers and designers"* (Exo 35:30–36).

Bezalel was said to be highly gifted as a workman, showing great skill and originality in engraving precious metals and stones and in wood-carving. He was also a master-workman, having many apprentices under him whom he instructed in the arts. According to Exodus, he was called and endowed by God to construct the tent of meeting and its furniture. All of this was accomplished by the infilling of the Holy Spirit.

It may also have been that most of these skills had disappeared among the Israelites because the slaves of Egypt would not have been required to possess such intricate levels of craftsmanship. In that case, the empowerment and revelation of the Spirit birthed a new creative capability. This is implied in Exodus 36:1: *"So Bezalel, Oholiab and every skilled person to whom the Lord has given skill and ability to know how to carry out all the work of constructing the sanctuary are to do the work just as the Lord has commanded."*

This is the first recorded infilling of the Holy Spirit. Where have we gone wrong with seeing only a few people as set apart for the work of God? He has called all of us in the marketplace at our daily tasks to be filled with His Holy Spirit to accomplish His tasks and be a witness for Him.

An encounter

I have made an assumption that may not be true. The vast majority of you who are reading this book will have had some kind of experience with God and regard yourselves as Christians. If that is not the case for you, then I would encourage you to persevere with this book because in its pages you may well find something beyond knowledge and understanding. You may find a loving heavenly Father who loves you with an undying, unending passion. He is a heavenly Father who will forgive you of anything you have done wrong and reconcile you to Himself. He also has a plan and purpose for your life and for all eternity. There is a nothing to lose and a lot to gain. Keep searching for the truth. It will ultimately become clear to you.

"For God so loved the world that he gave his one and only Son, that whoever believes in him shall not perish but have eternal life" (JOH 3:16).

This is what it is all about. Often familiarly breeds contempt. Take a moment to read the above verse with fresh eyes the familiar words with such poignant meaning. Jesus made the ultimate sacrifice and expression of an incomprehensible love that is so wide, so deep, and so complete that we cannot begin to understand its total, absolute, and monumental enormity. It is the perfect expression of perfect love.

"I pray that out of his glorious riches he may strengthen you with power through his Spirit in your inner being, so that Christ may dwell in your hearts through faith. And I pray that you, being rooted and established in love, may have power, together with all the Lord's holy people, to grasp how wide and long and high and deep is the love of Christ, and to know this love that surpasses knowledge—that you may be filled to the measure of all the fullness of God. Now to him who is able to do immeasurably more than all we ask or imagine, according to his power that is at work within us, to him be glory in the church and in Christ Jesus throughout all generations, for ever and ever! Amen" (EPH 3:16–21).

To those of you who have already had a revelation of who God is and have committed your lives to Him, how should this affect our view of work? Quite simply, our work life has to be laid on the foundation of an ongoing walk, and daily experience of God. It has to be based on an encounter with our heavenly Father.

"In reply Jesus declared, 'I tell you the truth, no one can see the kingdom of God unless he is born again'" (JOH 3:3 NIV1984).

You can only see the kingdom of God if you are born again. This occurs when we ask Jesus to forgive us and make Him Lord over our lives. Our spiritual eyes are then open, and we begin a journey of discovery in the kingdom.

Do you know you are going to heaven? Do you have an assurance that you are born again? You may have been around church all your life but not yet fully committed your life to Jesus. Why not make that decision today? You have a lot to gain.

If we want to have an effective walk with God in our workplace, the foundation has to be strong. Our work needs to be based on a genuine encounter and surrendered walk with our God. If we have invited God into our lives and have acknowledged Jesus and asked for His forgiveness, then it should be evidenced in our world. We need to become submitted to His will for our lives. He needs to be our Lord as well as our Savior. That is as valid in the marketplace as it is in all aspects of our walk with Him.

How tragic is it to hear so often, "I wouldn't do business with him, and he calls himself a Christian." Tragically, it is a travesty of all we claim to be and inoculates those who don't know Him to our message of hope and salvation. How we act at work has eternal consequences. Our God is unfortunately going to be judged by others in the light of the actions of those of us who are called to represent Him.

Surrender

If Jesus is truly the Lord of our lives, then He must be the Lord of our work. This therefore begs a couple of obvious questions: what does He want me to do, and how does He want me to do it? The roles we have and who we work for should be a call we hand over to God to make. What is His will, and how can we align ourselves to what He is doing?

Many years ago, I worked for a small company as a manager of a handful of people. The owner was—how shall I put it?—'different' and from my perspective, somewhat difficult. I struggled with his approach. The business had done well and had been turned around. There had been a good increase in profitability under a new strategy and the blessing of God. I wanted to move on, but I felt strongly that I needed to stay. Then along came a great job offer. My instant reaction was, *Great—here is an opportunity to escape from what looks like a dead end.* I felt this was the answer to my prayers that would release me from my burden.

However, I had already learned to take these things before God. When I did so, I felt that I was not supposed to accept the new job offer, but instead I was to stay and keep serving the owner of the business where I was employed. To say I felt disappointed was an understatement. I could see no way out, and the supposedly God-ordained answer was not meant to be taken.

I struggled with this a lot. Had I heard from God, or was it just me making it up? I definitely wanted to leave and take on this other role, but I could not feel peaceful about the situation. I eventually concluded I should stay. This was an act of reluctant surrender.

My conversion experience in my early twenties had taught me to put my trust in God and not in myself. Reluctantly, I went back to God and said to Him, "If You want to stay here for the rest of my life, serving this man, then so be it." I took out the proverbial big white flag of surrender and waved it before God. I prayed, "Your will be done, Lord, not mine."

The next day there an open letter was placed in my in tray in error. The business I was running was for sale, and a prospective buyer had been found. To make a long story short, the buyer was a company called Charles Parsons New Zealand Limited. It was a company I would eventually lead, and subsequently, after I left and returned later, I was asked to become the group managing director of its six-country group, with several hundred millions in turnover and with over one thousand staff members at its peak.

I might have missed out on all of these doors of opportunity if I had followed my own wishes and moved to another company. We need to be surrendered to God's purposes and to learn to lean not on our own understanding but trust Him who has our best in mind.

"Trust in the LORD with all your heart and lean not on your own understanding; in all your ways submit to him, and he will make your paths straight" (Pro 3:5–6).

As we reach out for God's purposes in our lives, He responds with tests and challenges for us to prove our obedience and trust in Him. When we submit to His ways and His will, He gives us the desires of our hearts. He is the one Who has placed passions and dreams within us. Often we endeavor to realize these in our own strength rather than submit them to Him and watch Him work it all out for good. Sometimes it is laying down of what we cherish that causes it to be ultimately fulfilled in our lives.

Stewardship

We have all been given something. It is something that is given in equal measure to everyone—something we all have exactly the same measure of every day. It is a limited, finite resource that is new every morning but gone every night: time. What a precious commodity it is.

Time is so easy to waste and so seemingly hard to redeem. It is an allocated allotment, fixed and finite. We also have talents, gifts, passions, and abilities. There are resources both physical and spiritual that are at our disposal. We have an obligation to deal wisely with what we have been given, and to exercise diligence, as well as wisdom in what we do with what we have.

"From everyone who has been given much, much will be demanded; and from the one who has been entrusted with much, much more will be asked" (LUK 12:48).

It is all His; we are merely stewards of what He has seen fit to give us. One day we will need to give account for what we have done with what we have been given. It is in the application of our talents at work that we have an opportunity to serve God, and His expects of a return on His investment in us. Everything we have comes from Him. It is only as we surrender ourselves to Him in the workplace that He can begin to use us to glorify Himself in our area of influence.

"To the Lord your God belong the heavens, even the highest heavens, the earth and everything in it" (DEU 10:14).

Everything; now there is an all-encompassing and all-containing word. There are no exceptions, no exclusions, and no special cases, and nothing is left out. It all belongs to God, whether we agree or not, accept or not, or believe or not. If it is in heaven, it is His, and if it is on earth, it is His. All we have, and all we think we own, is His. If this is true, then we are merely stewards of what belongs to God.

If we really thought about that and understood this fact in all its ramifications, would our lives be different? Perhaps we would be more generous, less frivolous, and more thankful. To begin with, perhaps we should acknowledge that God owns it all, and then maybe He will respond by giving us a greater revelation of how we should steward what is His.

Our attitude toward stewardship could easily become one of servitude. If our revelation of the Father's heart is not correctly formed, we could slip again into a doctrine of works, as if we could gain favor with God through works rather than purely by grace and faith. Works are merely the evidence of the faith within us.

God has saved us because He loves us, and we serve Him out of knowledge, understanding, and a revelation of that ridiculous, uncompromising, unending, unmerited love. It is a love that is so all encompassing that we can barely begin to even grasp one iota of its significance. As Paul wrote in Ephesians 3:17–18, *"And I pray that you, being rooted and established in love, may have power, together with all the Lord's holy people, to grasp how wide and long and high and deep is the love of Christ."*

The revelation of His love is based on being established in His love. It is a virtuous circle of revelation, empowerment, and further revelation. It is an unending resource of motivation and sense of purpose, which we can never ever exhaust because His love for us knows no bounds.

He is our Redeemer, and He has redeemed us for a purpose. As the Lord's Prayer so aptly puts it, *"Your kingdom come, your will be done."* In that small snippet that so many know so well is our mandate to transform our sphere of influence, our workplace, and the broader marketplace.

God is interested in the whole of our lives, not some small component of it, not a special day or a few hours, but all of it—all day, all week, all month, and for the rest of your life and on into eternity. The plan and purpose He has is for the complete, whole you on every day and in every way, all, complete, in totality, and in every minute detail.

You are redeemed, blessed, and called for a purpose. You are and will be equipped for all He is asking you to do. You are anointed with spiritual power, discernment, and gifts to bear fruit for Him, to establish His kingdom, and to be effective in your workplace. As Luke 19:13 says, *"So he called ten of his servants and gave them ten minas. 'Put this money to work,' he said, 'until I come back.'"*

God is intimately interested in all aspects of your work life. It is not an add-on or a way to provide. He has asked you to work and will show you how to work in ways you will not expect. Your ministry and calling is in the marketplace. Your mission field is your workplace; your pulpit is the role you hold. Expect God to guide and lead you just as a leader in a church is guided and led. There is no difference in the calling.

He wants you in business, and that is where you will be most effective and most fulfilled and where you will see His hand at work. Often we look to go elsewhere, but maybe God wants you to bloom where you are, to serve where you are, and to bless you where you are.

In the next few chapters, we will explore what it means to serve God in the workplace. We will look at how we can integrate our faith into our jobs. We will look at the ways God can use us to impact others for good—not only those around us but ourselves as well. We will explore how we can find God at work now that we understand that we are called, appointed, and anointed for a specific business purpose and that Monday matters.

Oh, and by the way, it is okay to relax and enjoy the journey.

Key Scripture

"The Lord God took the man and put Him in the Garden of Eden to work it and take care of it" (GEN 2:15).

Main Points

- There is no separation between sacred and secular.
- We are uniquely created for a specific purpose.
- Work is God's idea.
- God is intimately and passionately interested in our work.
- God is the owner of all we have.

Prayer

Father, thank You for work. I understand now that it is Your idea. Show me how to apply Your principles in my workplace. I yield once again to Your purposes and plans, especially at my workplace. Establish Your blessings in my work life so I may be effective in Your kingdom. In Jesus' name, Amen.

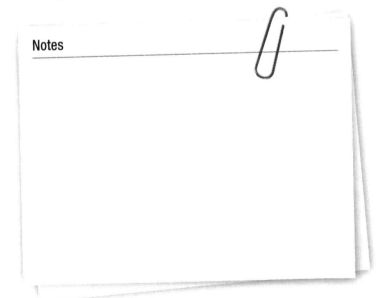

Notes

CHAPTER 2

WORK TO PROVIDE

*"God is able to make all grace abound to you, so that in
all things at all times, having all that you need, you will
abound in every good work"*

(2 COR 9:8 NIV1984).

Let's deal with the most obvious aspect of work first. God has ordained work as the method of His provision; we all know this to be true. No work means no pay, yet the mortgage has to be paid and the children taken care of. Now let's take a closer look at the seemingly obvious and explore God's provision through work.

Provision comes to us primarily in the form of a monetary reward. It is given to us in exchange for our labor or investment or perhaps the creative, entrepreneurial leverage of both in a business environment. We are expected to put our hand to the plough in some form or another to reap that reward.

Once we have received what is due to us, we have a God-given responsibility to steward God's resources wisely in their application and blessing. This blessing is not only for ourselves but also for those we are responsible for, for the work of God, and for the wider community. But before we delve a little deeper into this subject, let's spend some time considering something all of us spend a considerable amount of time earning, spending, and worrying about.

Money

What is it about Christians and money? For some it is seen as a sign of the world. They have a 'filthy lucre' perspective that portrays money as evil. This often comes with a 'poverty is a virtue' mentality that equates any level of material gain as somehow less than spiritual. In many cases, the opposite is also true. There are churches where God is obviously short again this week and needs some more of your money. Their focus on money is almost overwhelming and constant.

Then there is a balance where money is seen in its true context and monetary principles are taught in balance from a scriptural perspective and in accordance with a God-focused view. Jesus had a lot to say about money, and so should we. Is there anything wrong with having a few spare coins in your pocket? Absolutely not!

The Good Samaritan would have had a significant problem if he had been unable to pay for the man he helped. He paid for the beaten man's hotel stay in advance. He also had enough money that he was able to promise to come back and pay any extra required. That would have been a significant problem had his Bank of Samaria credit card been maxed out.

There are some wonderful Scriptures pertaining to this area. One of my absolute favorites, 2 Corinthians 9:8, says, *"God is able to make all grace abound to you, so that in all things at all times, having all that you need, you will abound in every good work."* What a wonderful promise of provision—a full sufficiency at all times to be able to do good works. God clearly links provision with being available to do good in this verse.

Also note that it is provided through His grace. We are at the mercy of God's goodness and grace. Regardless of all our efforts and application, everything comes from Him. Yes, we have to put our hand to the plow and apply a good, godly work ethic, but ultimately, He is the one Who gives us the ability and opportunity to grow wealth.

Income is, quite rightly, most people's primary motivation to work. There is nothing wrong with a motive of earning and providing. This is not an evil desire. After all, it is necessary to provide for those God has entrusted into our care. That is also why companies exist—to make a profit. No one starts a business intending for it to fail and go broke. A business does not need to exist for any higher spiritual reason or outcome than to earn and provide. This is of itself intrinsically good.

We need to understand this revelation because we are so used to seeing commercial areas through a segmented religious rather than a scriptural mindset. Let's not over-spiritualize the reasons we work. There is nothing wrong with a profit motive. There is nothing wrong with money. Money is a great tool. Money is morally neutral, neither good nor bad.

People often misquote Scripture to say, "Money is the root of all evil." The verse in question is 1 Timothy 6:10, and it correctly reads as follows: *"For the love of money is a root of all kinds of evil. Some people, eager for money, have wandered from the faith and pierced themselves with many griefs"* (NIV1984). The warning is abundantly apparent: it is the unshackled desire of our hearts—unfettered by the restraint that comes from a surrendered life—that ultimately brings destruction.

Profit

Money buys freedom of choice and options to give and sow into the work of the kingdom. We are often constrained because of lack and held back from doing a world of good by insufficient resources. It is time to not shrink back but to understand that God's provision, when sanctified and surrendered to His purposes, is a powerful and effective resource that we should harness and put to good use.

The question we should ask about profit is, "At what cost will you seek to attain it?" What checks and balances are in you and your business to constrain the wanton pursuit of profit at all costs? If that desire is not balanced, then it can get a hold of you and cause great grief. The Scripture mentioned previously talked of being "pierced with many sorrows." That is a picture of real pain, so it is important for us to be balanced and constrained in our handling of money.

There are many examples of well-meaning people who became so focused on monetary rewards that they lost sight of what was important, and their lives reflect the Scripture and are filled with "many sorrows." However—and let me put this in unequivocal terms, because we need to hear this loud and clear—there is nothing wrong with a profit motive. Companies exist intrinsically and essentially to make money. If a company purely exists for commercial purposes, it needs no other reason to justify its existence. We will look at how work is a godly pursuit in more detail later, but if work is ordained by God and has value to Him, then it stands to reason that the vehicle of work, in our democratic capitalist system, is inherently a good thing.

A healthy business not only grows but also increases its wealth and resources so it can accomplish more of what it exists to create. While a company is an inanimate concept, it does exist in the values and vision it is endowed with by its creators and leaders. In that sense, it has a perpetual mandate that can be for good or evil. It is, however—as is money—morally neutral. It is merely a tool, and its ownership and use designate its value, purpose, usefulness, and even sanctification.

Profit is not a four-letter word. It is a great motivator and a vital goal. It brings with it growth and investment, sustainability and employment. Our economies and collective community wealth are borne in the execution of commerce. God uses our labor and capital to provide for us to meet our needs and bless us. Our personal needs are met, we have provision for our families, and we can begin to bless others and meet their needs.

My definition of prosperity is this: *"All our needs met and enough to give away."* We are rich beyond all measure on any comparative world scale. All we have and all we are comes from the hand of God. The resources we enjoy, the profits we make, the wages we earn, and the experiences we have—they all come from Him and as such, they all are blessings.

Generosity

Giving moderates greed. These two opposing forces bring balance to our motivations. The discipline and exercise of giving will negate our natural, carnal propensity for greed. God calls us to a generous life, a giving life, as demonstrated by His Son, who gave His life for all humankind. The pursuit of wealth for wealth's sake will bring with it collateral damage in other areas of our lives if it is not counterbalanced with a generous spirit.

God is our provider. Provision is a part of His covenant with us. It is a reflection of who He is, a part of His very nature and character. He was called Jehovah-Jireh when He provided the ram in place of Isaac for Abraham's sacrifice in Genesis 22:14: *"So Abraham called that place The LORD Will Provide. And to this day it is said, 'On the mountain of the LORD it will be provided.'"* The meaning of Jehovah-Jireh is "The Lord Who Provides." The name is literally translated as "The Lord who sees."[4] He sees our needs and promises to provide.

So how do we embed this truth into our lives? There are biblical principles regarding giving, and certainly a recognition that all we have comes from the hand of God is a prerequisite understanding. I believe that we need to do two things.

First, we need to come before God and surrender this area of our lives to Him. That is not as easy to do as it sounds. Are we really willing to give up our sovereignty in this area? This is not a one-off event; it will be an area of sovereign risk, battle, and debate over a lifetime.

Second, we need to decide before Him what to give and to whom. Do this in private with an open heart. God is the one to Whom you will ultimately give account. Once decided, you need to honor that commitment. I have found if I operate in this way, I am more likely to give cheerfully and less likely to feel under compulsion. And judging by 2 Corinthians 9:7, God likes that: *"Each man should give what he has decided in his heart to give, not reluctantly or under compulsion, for God loves a cheerful giver."* Personally I find the discipline of putting aside a predefined, fixed amount every month into a dedicated account specifically for His purposes gives me the ability to give when a need arises and to regularly support what God lays on my heart.

"According to their ability they gave to the treasury for this work 61,000 darics of gold, 5,000 minas of silver and 100 priestly garments" (EZR 2:69).

---

4   *Knowing God by Name*, David Wilkerson, 2003, Baker.

We are all called to be a part of the solution according to our ability to give. We are called to give "according to our ability." It is not the amount in question but the heart of generosity behind the act. God will use the discipline and blessing of giving to change you and provide for His kingdom.

Giving may vary from time to time and season to season. This requires wisdom and an ability to discern and hear from God. Sometimes we are asked to give sacrificially. Counter to some modern preaching, every so often sacrifice actually means a sacrifice. We are sometimes called to go without.

It is unfortunate that some teaching about tithing has been combined with the principle of sowing and reaping. These are two separate and valuable principles that, when combined, can create a distorted view. This is a somewhat contentious opinion, but I would challenge you to look at the historical account of tithing and see if it really reflects the way it is being sold today.

In extreme cases, it is placing people under compulsion and creating false expectations and even bondage. While the vast majority of preaching on the subject is done with the best intentions by godly men and women, I believe it is an area where each of us should individually go to God, search His Word, and form our own view. When you do, check that your motivation is not to absolve yourself from giving or to ascertain a minimum but to seek the truth. To some He may well say, "Give it all away." It all belongs to Him, not just the 10 percent.

The rule for me is not a fixed sum or even a constant portion but a surrendered obedience given in freedom, not under compulsion, save for the graceful and generous conviction of the Holy Spirit. I would not like to eat what has been designated by God to give or give what was destined to bless my immediate family. This is a somewhat contentious area with a lot of dogma and in some cases unscriptural renderings of past principles. It is an area where we would do well not to take a view until we have looked to God for ourselves and discerned what He would have us do.

"One man gives freely, yet gains even more; another withholds unduly, but comes to poverty" (PRO 11:24).

In the world we are taught that if you are tight with your money, you will get more, yet the law of the kingdom is the opposite. Give and it will be given unto you. Withhold and you will come to poverty. It sounds upside down, but how often is that true with the things that God asks of us? He had to die to bring life. His death led to victory.

There is a wonderful passage in the Bible where Paul points to the attitude of a church that is a wonderful example of generosity. We should measure our motivation against the people of this congregation.

"And now, brothers and sisters, we want you to know about the grace that God has given the Macedonian churches. In the midst of a very severe trial, their overflowing joy and their extreme poverty welled up in rich generosity. For I testify that they gave as much as they were able, and even beyond their ability. Entirely on their own, they urgently pleaded with us for the privilege of sharing in this service to the Lord's people. And they exceeded our expectations: They gave themselves first of all to the Lord, and then by the will of God also to us" (2 COR 8:1–5).

Their generosity was borne in grace, refined in trial, and overflowing to go beyond their expectations of serving the Lord. There was no compulsion, just an extreme love leading to extreme generosity.

The Holy Spirit will encourage and guide us as we seek to work out the balance of a healthy drive for a successful business and the social, ethical, and moral imperatives, within which context the push for gain is contained and constrained. Moderation is a virtue, and God's principles of giving and sacrifice bring balance to our natural tendency for greed. A life free from all sorts of excess is a life well lived and lived well.

Our generosity should be to everyone without necessarily denigrating ourselves. There are times when we are undoubtedly called to go without, such as fasting or sacrificial giving, but as a default position, we need to be generous with ourselves. This gives us the ability to be generous to others, just as a healthy self-awareness and esteem frees us to love and understand those around us.

Personal Need

God provides for us personally by giving us abilities to serve and meet the needs, wants, and desires of others. The provision we receive for our labors and investment are for many purposes: to bless us, our families, the work of the kingdom, the poor, and others we are called to support.

"Command those who are rich in this present world not to be arrogant nor to put their hope in wealth, which is so uncertain, but to put their hope in God, who richly provides us with everything for our enjoyment" (1 Tim 6:17).

You may not consider yourself to be rich, but what is your opinion based on? To whom do you compare yourself? Have you seen the images from Africa? If you are able to read this book, then you are in the top few in the world—a world where many starve and barely live. From God's perspective, He can see it all.

We are rich. Therefore, this Scripture applies to us. Let us not be arrogant. Let us not put our hope in wealth. Yes, we are indeed so wealthy. It is very easy to trust in a pay packet and a good business, an investment, or even the somewhat volatile stock market. We trust in our savings, houses, and superannuation. These are all good things—very good things—yet our attitude should recognize that they are uncertain, temporal, and a mere vapor, compared to an enduring, faithful God. It is in Him that we place our trust and have our hope. When we do that, we will be able to enjoy what He has so richly blessed us with.

He provides it for our enjoyment, so let's not get too pious and super-spiritual that we downgrade our enjoyment of all our heavenly Father has seen fit to give to us. He understands completely the society and situation into which He has placed us. He wants His salt and light to be experienced by all strata, sectors, segments, and social positions in every society and community. He will place His people to influence others for good and will equip them accordingly with the resources necessary to complete the task. He is neither stingy nor tight. He is a generous God.

It is important to not only accept and enjoy what He has given us but to find our contentment in more than just income. We have all succumbed to one degree or another to the never-ending consumerism of the next model or the latest and greatest. I seem to have an insatiable appetite for the next 'must-have' gadget. It is important as we discuss personal need that the desire for what constitutes a need is put into the correct perspective.

"I know what it is to be in need, and I know what it is to have plenty. I have learned the secret of being content in any and every situation, whether well fed or hungry, whether living in plenty or in want" (Phi 4:12).

What is true contentment? What would it take for you to feel truly content? We tend to think of contentment in terms of material possessions, relationships and circumstances. Paul, who was shipwrecked, beaten, stoned, and jailed, amongst other great experiences, is talking about something much deeper. There is a peace that goes beyond all understanding, beyond circumstances and experiences. It is a contentment that can only be supernatural in origin. When Paul wrote these words to the Philippians, he was in jail. This was a jail in a basement where sewage flowed from the building and through his cell, where he was chained by the hands. He was released only for a few hours a day. I am not sure I would be writing about joy under those circumstances. The perspective Paul had was above circumstances, not under them.

Imagine being so close to God that all else pales into insignificance. Everything truly becomes a shadow in the context of the all-powerful light of a totally radiant God. The closer we get to Him, the more content we will be. He is the only certainty, the only constant, and the only place of true contentment.

What a great place to be—totally content. It is okay to enjoy what has come from His hand. The closer we get to Him, the more objective we become about what our needs may be and the less reliant we become on our wants to satisfy our desires.

"Because the Lord your God will bless you in all your produce and in all the work of your hands, so that you surely rejoice" (DEU 16:15).

Enjoy what God has given you. He has blessed you so you may bless others but also so you will rejoice. Relax and enjoy the blessings of God. He enjoys seeing you blessed, just as we as earthly, worldly parents love to see our children or others blessed by what we give them.

God has said He will bless our produce and the work of our hands. Expect to see His hand at work in your work. He does and will always provide for you as you work according to His principles and tenets.

Families' needs

Can we now move on from personal blessing to considering others? Despite the fact that most of us are under the illusion that the world rotates around us, it is, as Rick Warren has so famously written, "not about you." He goes on to say, "*The purpose of your life is far greater than your own personal fulfillment, your peace of mind, or even your happiness.*"[5]

What are our priorities? Our next priority and ministry after the ministry to ourselves is to our immediate family and the provision required to meet their needs. God certainly puts

---

5 *The Purpose-Driven Life*, Rick Warren, 2004, Zondervan.

high regard on providing for our families, as He says in 1 Timothy 5:8, *"Anyone who does not provide for their relatives, and especially for their own household, has denied the faith and is worse than an unbeliever."* That is a serious indication of the importance God places on us providing for our families. It is a responsibility we would do well to take seriously into account. In a world where careers and business take a big toll on families, we need to be very mindful not only of the physical provision but also the spiritual and emotional needs of those nearest and dearest to us.

Beyond ourselves, this is our primary ministry, and as such, it should receive the largest share of our generosity and service. Too often I have seen families sacrificed on the basis of doing "God's work." We need to understand that we minister daily in our workplace and in our families. While we have an obligation for corporate service and for participation in and commitment to organized community, that commitment needs to be in conjunction with a healthy, objective perspective on ministry priority.

We are called to be generous with our families, just as we should be generous with ourselves and with others. Our families should not get just the leftovers from our lives when all else is done. I have found that when I invest in my family, I am released for service elsewhere, safe in the knowledge that they are being well cared for and satisfied emotionally, physically, and spiritually. Our generosity should be like God's generosity at home, in the workplace, and in all our areas of ministry and service.

"So Simon Peter climbed back into the boat and dragged the net ashore. It was full of large fish, 153, but even with so many the net was not torn" (JOH 21:11).

I love this Scripture for two quite distinct reasons. First, God is an abundant provider. The nets weren't full of just enough for the day. There was more than a sufficient amount and well beyond the minimum requirement. The provision went well beyond satisfying any need. God's motivation in provision is to more than satisfy our needs by going beyond our expectations.

In addition to oversupplying the need, they weren't just normal, small, average, everyday fish; they were "large"—big, fat, juicy, large fish, and they came in abundance. This is God's economy in action, a specific example of His style of provision.

Is this what we expect for our workplaces and for the provision for our families? Why not? Are we not in God's service? Are we not serving and a part of His family? Is He not the same yesterday, today, and forever? What applied then applies now. He does not change as time progresses; He is outside of time and eternal.

"Jesus Christ is the same yesterday and today and forever" (HEB 13:8).

The second aspect of this Scripture that often goes unmentioned is that despite this massive haul of fish, the nets were not damaged. God can enlarge our capacity for a harvest, whether that is financially or as fishers of men. Our families, our businesses, and we can become the vessels that can contain the abundance of all God has for us. If He gives us an 'over and above' provision, He will ensure we are capable of handling all He provides.

Others' needs

God has another focus for our prosperity and His provision that goes beyond our immediate families and us. Remember that whatever we have been given has come from His hand. He has the right and has the ability to call on what He wants for His purposes.

"But who am I, and who are my people, that we should be able to give as generously as this? Everything comes from you, and we have given you only what comes from your hand" (1 CHR 29:14).

God gives us excess so we will be able to give. He does this to demonstrate His love to others. We are merely following the pattern of His heart and generosity to us. He is the ultimate giver who gave us His Son. All we have is His. Let's hold on to it gently, knowing that He may have uses for it elsewhere, and be faithful as stewards of all He has given us.

We are called to look out for those who are in need and for them to see and experience the provision and message our lives should be demonstrating. As Philippians 2:4 says, *"Not looking to your own interests but each of you to the interests of the others."* As we give to those around us who are in need, we will see an impact for God. It will be seen as a demonstration of God's hand at work, and we need to ensure it is done in such a way that He gets the glory, not us. When it is done in the right spirit and under the unction of God, the fruit we should experience is thanksgiving to God.

"You will be enriched in every way so that you can be generous on every occasion, and through us your generosity will result in thanksgiving to God" (2 COR 9:11).

It is interesting to note that this Scripture doesn't say we can be generous on some occasions or even most occasions but on every occasion. How can we do that? We can do it because we will be enriched to be able to do so. Why? So that thanksgiving will be given to God.

This principle should be applied in all aspects of our giving. We need to be a part of a local community and plugged into a local church. The operating of such and the provision for those chosen to teach and pastor is our responsibility. They are there to equip us for works of service and should be honored and provided for well. We need to get rid of the poisonous notion that keeping church leaders and fulltime workers on the poverty line somehow makes them more pious. It is one of the worst abuses of religiosity and should be relegated to history. What an asinine concept. It is truly repugnant and totally counters the revelation of a generous God.

If you have read much of the Bible at all, it is obvious that God has a heart for the poor. The way He describes true, pure, and faultless religion should not be a surprise. Does he describe it as pious, righteous people in pews who are well dressed in wonderful church buildings? No, God sees pure religion in another way, as described in James 1:27: *"Religion that God our Father accepts as pure and faultless is this: to look after orphans and widows in their distress and to keep oneself from being polluted by the world."*

We are called to fund the work of God and to balance our greed with living a generous life. We need to be disciplined and open to God's leading in our giving of finances and time. As a body of Christ we should strive for a responsible balance before God and one not tainted by our Western, consumer oriented, materialistic need, for instant gratification.

"Do not store up for yourselves treasures on earth, where moths and vermin destroy, and where thieves break in and steal. But store up for yourselves treasures in heaven, where moths and vermin do not destroy, and where thieves do not break in and steal. For where your treasure is, there your heart will be also" (MAT 6:19–21).

Here is a sobering and somewhat disturbing thought. Imagine if God has kept a record of all our checks, automatic payments, and credit card transactions. Would He be pleased with the evidence of what our priorities were? Conversely, if they were taken as a record and used as evidence against you on the charge of being a Christian, would there be enough evidence to convict you? What is our perspective, and how do we allocate the provision we have received? These are tough questions but ones well worth considering.

If we take an eternal perspective, looking down in a couple of hundred years or so, what would be important? Is it the temporal, instant satisfaction of the latest toy or gadget or perhaps the eternal souls affected by an investment in a mission, a gift, a ministry supported, a church planted, or a soul won?

There is a reward for kingdom investment—a reward with eternal value. As the great song *Amazing Grace* says,

"When we've been there ten thousand years,
bright shining as the sun, we've no less days
to sing God's praise than when we first begun."

That is a great perspective. What a wonderful view of eternity, for our earthly life is so short compared with endless eons. We are just a whisper, a shadow, a vapor, and a passing moment in history.

The comparative value of what we do and the prospective reward for what we do, as well as how we spend and where we invest, should reflect our understanding of the temporal nature of our earthly existence. We would do well to consider our decisions with an eternal perspective.

We work in order to earn money, but that provision comes from God. It is He who provides and we have a responsibility to minister with the provision we receive. We are to be generous in accordance with God's character and example; firstly to ourselves, and our family, and then to others, the poor and for the advancement of God's kingdom. We are called to be wise in our giving and investment, to decide in our hearts what to give and to give cheerfully, not under compulsion. All this is to be done with an eternal perspective that brings balance and Godly reason to our use and stewardship of His providence.

Key Scripture

"And God is able to make all grace abound to you, so that in all things at all times, having all that you need, you will abound in every good work" (2 Cor 9:8 NIV1984).

Main Points

- All you are and all you have come from Him.
- God provided work for you to work to provide.
- There is nothing wrong with money.
- Profit is a good thing.
- Generosity balances greed.

Prayer

Father, I acknowledge that You are my provider and that all that I have is Yours. Teach me to be generous, and open my eyes to see what You are doing around me and the part You want me to play. Thank You for using work to provide for my, my family's, and others' needs. I will be faithful in my stewardship with Your help, in Jesus' name. Amen

Notes

CHAPTER 3
WORK TO GROW

"And we, who with unveiled faces all reflect the Lord's glory, are being transformed into his likeness with ever-increasing glory, which comes from the Lord, who is the Spirit"

(2 COR 3:18 NIV1984).

Growth is a natural outcome of anything that is healthy and in the right environment. In this chapter, we will explore how God can use your work environment to grow you as a person. Psalm 139:16 says, *"All the days ordained for me were written in your book before one of them came to be."*

If He plans every day, I am sure that He has included Monday through Friday. I also surmise it would include the hours between 8.00am and 6.00pm. If that is the case, then God's plan will be worked out while we are at work. If you have not thought about God's interest in your work, just consider the possibility, invite Him into your workplace, and watch His will begin to unfold. He will transform both you and those around you.

Character

I have some bad news for you: God is more interested in your character than your prosperity! Much though we would like to leave our work in the realm of earning and provision, it has much more to deliver than dollars. While He is interested in our fiscal wellbeing and provision, His purposes, as usual, go much deeper.

If He is for us, why do we often we find ourselves battling? This is particularly true at work. We spend a lot of time working, and a lot of it can be a grind. Life can be tough, and this is true for our work as well as life in general. God has an agenda—a loving agenda. He has us on a program. He has a plan to grow us in stature and character so we can become more like Him.

Have you had trouble at work? Maybe it is a difficult boss or colleagues. Things do go wrong at work, but why? God will use your work to bring about personal transformation. God will use your work to put pressure on you to shape and mold you into His image. We need to begin to recognize the hand of God in the valleys as well as on the mountaintops. He is changing us as we respond in faith to what He is doing and asking us to do.

"So all of us who have had that veil removed can see and reflect the glory of the Lord. And the Lord—who is the Spirit—makes us more and more like him as we are changed into his glorious image" (2 Cor 3:18 NLT).

We need to learn to hear and heed that still, quiet voice. We need to press into Him and hear what He is saying in the circumstances in which we find ourselves. Often we are to stand in faith and claim the promises of God. Some promises of God have to be appropriated by faith as we trust Him and stand on His Word. Answers can come quickly, but sometimes we are to persevere and persist—to endure and to overcome in stages.

It is our reaction to the situations and circumstances in which we find ourselves that begins to shape and mold us. None of us would choose to be placed under pressure, but there are no diamonds without pressure. None of us would want to be put in the fire of trials, but gold cannot be refined without fire. As it is in the natural, so it is in the spiritual. The trials and tribulations we face will produce enduring fruit if we yield and respond appropriately.

The situations that could cause bitterness, resentment, and hatred with a carnal response produce patience, perseverance, and love when yielded to God and responded to as He would have us respond.

Understanding that He has our greatest good in mind and that He wants to shape us allows us to search Him out in all we see and experience. There is no better place to do this than at work. The opportunities for shaping us daily are all to obviously available to Him.

"All his brothers and sisters and everyone who had known him before came and ate with him in his house. They comforted and consoled him over all the trouble the Lord had brought on him, and each one gave him a piece of silver and a gold ring" (Job 42:11).

This is a somewhat challenging Scripture because it seems to indicate that God was causing the trouble. I am not sure that fits in with my "come-to-Jesus-and-everything-will-be-wonderful" theology. Unfortunately, or perhaps more correctly, fortunately, God is bigger than our image of Him and of our attempts to put Him in a box. We may have experienced, understood, and adopted the milk of the word, but this one is more like the broccoli of the word. It is probably good for you but not a great experience. The Lord will allow all sorts of things to befall us. We need to understand the difference between what needs to be submitted to and endured, what needs our persistence to overcome, and what is an attack that needs to be repelled.

Our first ministry is to God; it is from Him we receive all we need to operate effectively. He is our source of all things that are good. Guarding our personal devotional life is critical to minister into all the areas in which He has given authority. Intimacy with Him will empower and anoint us to move effectively in our world. When we read the Bible and pray, the combination of the Word and the Holy Spirit creates revelations that will literally transform our lives.

Our guide and measure in all this is the Bible, the Word of God. It is our measure and standard. When we read it, empowered with the understanding of the Holy Spirit, it is quickened to our spirits. It is the only book that reads us as we read it. I cannot overemphasize the need to study the Word daily and prayerfully so we can understand what God is doing and how we should respond to the circumstances and challenges we experience every day.

To get that level of understanding, we need an ongoing relationship with God to lead and guide us. If the experience of trouble has been sanctioned from heaven, learn well and surrender fast; it's a much easier journey. Usually these adverse circumstances are created by us or someone else; occasionally we get true demonic opposition. Discernment of a cause is important. But regardless of the circumstances, God will turn it all to His purposes and our good as we seek to respond in His ways. It is all for our good, training us to rely on Him, to hear from Him, and ultimately to become more like His Son.

I have yet more bad news for you. There is no business transformation without personal transformation. If we lead a company or have any level of influence in one, it will become a reflection of who we are. Our character, our values, and the culture we inspire will pervade our organizations. Culture comes from the top, good or bad. We can articulate our desired values as much as we want, but our company's culture is caught, not taught. There is a wonderful Italian saying that says, "The fish rots from the head." How true that is. When you want to understand a company's culture, go and talk to its leader.

I have spent a lot of time in dysfunctional organizations that have gotten themselves into trouble. Many of my appointments have been to lead and turn around struggling companies. Often when companies that are not performing well assess themselves, the blame is leveled at the workers. Often they are the ones who pay the price for the incompetence and ineptitude foisted upon them as the legacy of bad management. I have found that it is almost always a lack of leadership that will take a company into troubled waters. When restructuring, I always look first to the team at the top. Often the ones who led a company into trouble are not the best ones to lead them out.

Companies rise to the level of leadership. John Maxwell aptly describes the five levels of leadership and is a strong proponent of the idea that a company can only rise to the level of its leader. I agree entirely. John Maxwell has also said, "Leaders become great, not because of their power, but because of their ability to empower others."[6]

This principle applies regardless of your position in a company. We all have a level of influence and authority. Often that is not

---

6   *The 5 Levels of Leadership,* John C. Maxwell, 2011, Center Street.

positional, as in your title, but is a result of the relationships you have with those around you. There is a big difference between positional, hierarchical power and personal power. I believe that personal power is honed by yielding to God's dealing with us. As this grows in us, He opens opportunities that may well come with positional power. If you want to grow in influence and opportunity, listen to God, and get onto His program.

Discipline

God will provide the situations we need to react to so we can grow and be transformed by His grace as we yield in obedience to His will. But this calls for more than passivity on our part. We need to establish a level of discipline in our lives to lay a platform for Him to operate effectively.

As with every aspect of life, it is our responsibility to ensure we are well disciplined and well trained to be able to operate efficiently and effectively. Those mundane daily routines are what lay down a strong platform from which we can grow. Often we are looking for the fruit even before we have taken the time to plant the seeds and water the plant. Fruit is a natural outcome if we have prepared the ground well, planted the seeds, watered and fed the plant, protected it when it was young, and took the time to tend, prune, and care for the tree. You can't get fruit straight from a seed; it just takes time and effort.

Discipline is such an important part of our lives. Without discipline, we become, unsurprisingly, undisciplined. Bringing into balance all the different aspects of our lives and putting in place boundaries and regular behaviors is critical if we are going to live a life where we have significant impact.

We are body, mind, and spirit, yet sometimes the segmentation is overestimated and oversimplified. Despite these different parts being described separately, we are still an integrated whole, and these aspects impact and interrelate with each other. If our body isn't being well fed and exercised, then our mind becomes impacted, and if our mind is impacted, then our spirit is impacted. The reverse is also true.

Sickness can be psychosomatic. If we are depressed, our minds don't function well. When we don't exercise, we can become disillusioned and not sharp. All these factors play on the other aspects of who we are. We are an integrated whole.

It is worth taking some time to look at the foundations we need to be able to function effectively.

Prayer

We have a call to intimacy and a daily walk with Jesus based on pressure at work that should drive us to be disciplined in prayer as well as in reading and studying the Word. It is human nature to call on God in times of trouble. There are no atheists in foxholes. When we are under stress, we call out for some help. If we have laid a platform of regular prayer and times of contemplation, we have a base from which to work. Our prayer can truly be a two-way conversation—a trusting relationship based on familiarity and intimacy. Often the answers we need are given to us ahead of time.

I have a good friend who is way more disciplined than I am. He is always up early, and I mean really early. I am, I must confess, not a morning person. I encourage my friend to pray for me before I get up. It was great to hear that one early morning he was in fervent prayer walking in a park when the police confronted him. He had been a little too loud in his praising of God and been reported as a possible fundamentalist fanatic, which, of course, he is. An interesting conversation ensued with the understanding but slightly confused policeman.

We are all different and wired in diverse ways. However, we all do have a responsibility to find a time to set aside for Him and Him alone that suits our personality and wiring. It should be a time to say thanks, hear from heaven, and shift our hearts to align with Him and His purposes.

Our daily walk needs to be an ongoing conversation, one of a close relationship. God is interested in all we do at work. Prayer can unleash His wisdom and blessing. We can literally take what is in the spiritual and bring it to impact our physical work life by spending time in prayer. You may well be staggered by the results. He can move in ways that will astound us if we would just ask. As James 4:2 says, *"You do not have because you do not ask of God."*

Word

Reading the Bible is another foundational discipline that will help shape who we are and how effective we are in working out our purpose in life and in particular at work. Regular study of God's Word should be a priority for all followers of Jesus. It is God's love letter to us and is the only book that reads us as we read it. Hebrews 4:12 says, *"For the word of God is alive and active. Sharper than any double-edged sword, it penetrates even to dividing soul and spirit, joints and marrow; it judges the thoughts and attitudes of the heart."*

Reading in a spirit of listening and expectancy under the guidance of the Holy Spirit can be a life-changing practice. I always ask God to reveal His Word to me and to speak while I am reading. Often I am led to a particular Scripture or something really strikes me. I take this as something I should give attention to and have learned to take seriously what is said. God is practical in the sense that there is often an application in what He is telling us. We need to put into practice what we have heard. The value is not in the perception but in the application.

"But the man who looks intently into the perfect law that gives freedom, and continues to do this, not forgetting what he has heard, but doing it—he will be blessed in what he does" (JAM 1:25 NIV1984).

I read one chapter of my Bible a night as a matter of course and find that a great comfort and leveler. It centers me before I sleep. Others, like my aforementioned friend, prefer an earlier start, bearing in mind, of course, the valuable warning that the early worm gets the bird. Regardless of timing, the practice is a powerful one that will stand you in good stead.

I found myself in Tokyo during a very large earthquake. Mercifully, we were spared the devastation experienced by the accompanying tsunami further north. When I eventually made it to the airport, which was in lockdown, we were still experiencing many aftershocks. I sat down and took out my Bible to read a chapter as usual, and the chapter I was up to was Revelation 16, including the great earthquake."

"Then there came flashes of lightning, rumblings, peals of thunder and a severe earthquake. No earthquake like it has ever occurred since mankind has been on earth, so tremendous was the quake. The great city split into three parts, and the cities of the nations collapsed" (Rev 16:18–19).

The earth was literally shaking as I was reading. That was one Bible study I will never forget. It hammered home the realization that we are in a time of grace where people have an opportunity to repent and be forgiven. However, the time is short. One day this world will be wrapped up, and there will be no more time to get right with God. A time of judgment is coming.

We have talked a little about prayer. I am sure you understand the need to read and study the Word of God. However, there is a big difference between just reading and 'shopping list' prayer and, intimacy with God. One comes out of a sense of duty or need, the other out of a heartfelt love and desire for our heavenly Father. There is almost a catch-22 where intimacy is born out of intimacy. The more time we spend with God, the more intimate the relationship becomes.

The goal of all discipline is laying a foundation for an outcome. In this case, prayer and studying the Word of God are about moving into an intimate relationship with God. It is said that the longest distance in the world is between the head and the heart. How true that is.

Ultimately, we need to have in intimate experience with Jesus where we hear from God on a day-to-day basis. Our experience with God need not be confined to our quiet time; rather, it can be a daily and hourly walk. While we need to maintain the discipline of having time set aside, it is an ongoing, continuous walk and intimate experience of Him, hour by hour, that is our ultimate goal and with which we will become most effective.

Health

There are other aspects of a strong, disciplined foundation that may not seem very spiritual. Thanks to our logical Greek philosophical heritage, we have rendered our minds and spirits to be higher than our bodies. Yet we need to look after our bodies if we want to be effective for God at work.

Let's not get so super spiritual that we forget that God has given us a body to look after. We are told that we are temples of the Holy Spirit. We should be mindful not put an extension onto the Temple. Nor allow it to crumble into a state of disrepair. There is a saying, healthy mind healthy body. It is equally true to say healthy body, healthy mind.

"Do you not know that your bodies are temples of the Holy Spirit, who is in you, whom you have received from God? You are not your own; you were bought at a price. Therefore honor God with your bodies" (1 COR 6:19–20).

I am sure when you started reading this book, you didn't think I would proffer advice on what to eat. I am no expert by any means. However, the simple truth is that some of the disciplines that make us effective at work and allow God to grow us into all we can be are seemingly simple and mundane. They are not only for the mind and spirit but also for the body.

What I have learned is that one of the most fundamental spiritual principles is that we reap what we sow. It is a very simple concept and the essence of so much spiritual truth. Getting the right nutrition enables our bodies to work optimally. A healthy lifestyle, with good food, great exercise, and a healthy work-life balance, will ensure not only our longevity and sustainability, but it will also give us an effective base from which to minister in the workplace.

We all know most the basics, yet there is a billion-dollar business in diet books. Why? We are all looking for a quick fix, yet the fundamentals are known to us all. It is a case of calories in and calories out. If we eat too much and lead a sedentary life, we will gain weight and become unfit. That leads us to be ineffective in faith and in works.

God is interested in our bodies. He created them. He knows how they run, your individual needs, and how your specific body functions. If this is an area you struggle in, don't feel guilty, but ask God to help you put in place disciplines that will help ensure you live a long and effective life and achieve all He has called you to do. Many people haven't fulfilled their full calling because of poor discipline in this often-neglected area.

The rules are as fundamental as they are simple. Avoid refined, over-processed foods, too many saturated fats, and too much sugar. Prefer lean proteins, and keep carbohydrates in balance. Lots of fruits and vegetables will do you good. Drink plenty of water, and I find that eating most things in moderation brings good balance. Portion size as well as food type selection can really help. If you need help in this area, don't be afraid to ask. If you've come a long way from where you view ideal to be, just take one step closer, make one small change, and begin a journey back to the state that God intended.

If I am talking about food and health, then I cannot move on without talking about fitness. We seem to be polarized into different camps here: either a fanatical drive to become as fit as we can or abstinence from anything that raises the heartbeat over 120. There does need to be a balance. Again, I am no expert, but I do understand that a healthy body needs to be exercised regularly.

We all lead busy lives, and it is a challenge to build regular exercise into our regime. However, exercise is an essential part of maintaining our wellbeing and therefore our effectiveness in what God has called us to do. Again, please hear me. It is not my intention to arouse any sense of guilt but to challenge you to lay a foundation in your life that will not only bring balance and blessing to you personally but will also make you effective in the kingdom of God.

If we are to be witnesses and testimonies for God's goodness, maybe we need to look the part as well. That is not succumbing to a shallow, commercial, and false Western ideal body shape. But it is a commitment and acknowledgment that God is the Savior of our body as well as our mind, will, and spirit.

There is a massive industry around the whole area of fitness. We are spoiled with options and knowledge. We all know what we need to do. Yet buying the book, watching the DVD, joining the gym, or collecting yet another piece of exercise equipment will achieve nothing. With all knowledge, it is in the execution and application that will reap the rewards.

Believe me when I say I am not a big fan of exercise, but I do recognize a need to exercise frequently. If you can manage twenty minutes today, your job is done. If you can mix up some cardiovascular exercise with some light strength and muscle work, this is all you need to do. Even thirty minutes of exercise three times a week will maintain, if not improve, your fitness levels.

When you care for your body, eat the right foods, and do some regular exercise, you feel a lot better. Your mind is sharper and more engaged, you're more effective in your relationships, and you have a heightened sense of awareness.

Bringing these things into a structured, disciplined routine in your life will lay a foundation for real spiritual growth. Doing these things is actually an act of worship in itself. If our bodies are the temples of the Holy Spirit, then maintenance and oversight are an act of worship.

Fellowship

We have dealt so far with foundational aspects to help you grow at work based on you as an individual, but what about other people? Fellowship is such a quaint term. It is a word that seems to come from a different time, yet embedded in this old-world word is a truth that holds such power. We live in a society that exalts the individual. Our sense of community has devolved and been diluted significantly in our modern times, yet our connectedness is such an important part of what makes us effective. Community in its true sense brings completeness. We are not designed to be alone. As Genesis 2:18 says, *"The LORD God said, 'It is not good for the man to be alone.'"*

I would like to reiterate where I stand on church. This is because there are many misconceptions about marketplace ministry and the role the local church has to play. May I say unequivocally that I am a great supporter of the local church? While I see changes coming in the way the local church operates, it is an important aspect of what is necessary to lead a Christ-centered life.

We are encouraged and equipped as we meet together with others who have had the experience of meeting Jesus. An isolated walk is a dangerous one. In community we can learn and grow together, worship together, and hear from those who are gifted to teach and preach. It is an opportunity to serve one another and share in communion, in all the senses of that word.

The Scriptures are very clear in Ephesians 4:11–12 that the role of pastors and teachers is to equip the saints for works of service: *"So Christ himself gave the apostles, the prophets, the evangelists, the pastors and teachers, to equip his people for works of service, so that the body of Christ may be built up until we all reach unity in the faith and in the knowledge of the Son of God and become mature, attaining to the whole measure of the fullness of Christ."*

It is we the people—the laity, the pew sitters—who are to be taught, equipped, encouraged, and prepared to do the works of service. We have the responsibility to respond and be effective in the work of the Master Craftsman and do His bidding.

Those works of service are not a duplication of what the fivefold ministers do. They equip, and we serve. We serve in our businesses, our workplaces, our schools, and our everyday places where God has ordained us to be. It is in that process that we the body, the people, the church will be built up in unity and ultimately mature into the fullness of Christ.

Michael Baer wrote the book *Business as Mission*. I had the privilege of meeting him when he spoke at the 'Cre8 Conference' in Sydney, Australia, where I was the emcee. He gave a wonderful analogy of a rugby game. It has been adapted for local consumption from what we call American football. He aptly described the church as a game where, "there are 30 people on the field in desperate need of rest and 50,000 people in the stands in desperate need of exercise." What a wonderful picture—albeit slightly unfortunate—of us in the church.

Let us not succumb to what some are talking about, where the local church is abandoned so we can embrace a new model. It is not a case of 'either' or but of 'both and.' Yes, the local church needs to become less insular, and yes, we need to turn the model upside down, with people being released into their missions and ministries outside of the church context. But let's not throw the baby out with the bathwater. The church is a vital part of our Christian walk and experience, and it always will be.

In Hebrews 10:24–25, the Bible says, *"And let us consider how we may spur one another on toward love and good deeds, not giving up meeting together, as some are in the habit of doing, but encouraging one another."*

Christians are not built for isolation, much though some of us would like that to be the case. God places us in situations where others can impact our lives and we theirs. It is in our coming together where the power lies. It is in our connectedness that we are effective. Let us come together in unity of purpose and identity to be effective in our communities. Sunday is a wonderful opportunity to come together in corporate worship, to listen to the word being preached, to be built up, to have fellowship with one another, to minister to one another, and to be released again into the workplace where we work out our faith and ministry.

Accountability

One very important reason for Christians to meet together is to bring a level of accountability. As individuals, we are at risk not only of deception but also of temptation. Having people in our lives who can hold us accountable is a safety net to ensure that when we are under pressure, there are people around us to support us. This accountability is not only for our protection but also for our growth. It is a blessing to have a handful of people who are willing to talk into our lives, to encourage us, and to build us up, and who are not afraid to say what they think and are willing to bring correction when necessary.

I would encourage you to find a few people—not many, even just a couple—to share this walk of life with you. I have a number of these people in my life with whom I am transparent and who walk alongside me. As Proverbs 27:17 says, *"As iron sharpens iron, so one person sharpens another."* I have found that word to be true. There are seasons in my life when I talk into someone else's life, and seasons where they talk into mine.

It is very easy to be distracted and deceived. We have a very real enemy who is capable of picking us off, should we allow him to do so. Being a loner and an isolated individual outside of a corporate responsibility and accountability makes us vulnerable. While we may have confidence in our relationship with God and with our lives in general, we are nonetheless reliant on other people to speak into our lives. We all have blind spots, and they are called blind spots for a reason: we can't see them. There is humility in allowing a level of accountability. We all need it, whether we like to acknowledge it or not.

"So He called him in and asked him, 'What is this I hear about you? Give an account of your management, because you cannot be manager any longer'" (Luke 16:2).

God will call us to account. It is a spiritual principle and one that we would do well to place an emphasis on. We all need to be accountable to someone. Pick well and wisely, and allow God to bring these people into your life.

Work / Life Blend

I often get asked this question: how do you manage to do all that you do? I have worked as a CEO and managing director in fairly large companies. I sit on a number of not-for-profit boards and a commercial board, and I am actively engaged in leadership and industry bodies. My life is busy at home, where I am fortunately blessed with a wonderful wife and three great children. With Called to Business, I write and speak and am very active with blogs and other social media. I also do numerous other things that consume my spare time.

I'm giving you the overview to say that I am not unfamiliar with the challenges of balancing work and life. Life is busy and challenging. It is always a battle to maintain priorities and disciplines, and the things that demand my attention vary and change all the time.

So how do we address this problem? How do we get to all the things we need to do yet balance all the different aspects of our lives? There is no easy answer, yet there are some principles I have found to be effective in managing all the varied things that pull and compete for my attention.

Trying to get the balance in your life when there is so much pressure from so many places is almost impossible. In a lot of ways, the word balance may not be the right term. Yes we have to judge priorities against all the competing factors in our lives, but often it is an option to blend as opposed to balance. In today's world where we have 24-hour communication—technology that was only a dream a few years ago—and a requirement of availability in many commercial roles, there is no option other than to blend.

Why not go to a game or athletic tournament your child is in on Wednesday at 2.00? Then maybe at 8.00 that night you can send a few e-mails to Europe or Asia. The concept of balance to me is not so much a rigid time allocation but more an awareness of priorities. Planning your time and being ruthless with schedules can significantly improve your productivity. It is a matter of considering the problem and allocating the resources as required.

Vision

In trying to sort out the balance of competing priorities, it is important to start with fundamentals. What you want? What is important to you? Do have a vision for your life? Do you have burning ambitions and passions that are driving you in a particular direction? What are you willing to give up to achieve your goals? What do you believe God has for your life?

These are life-forming questions that need to be taken before God. He is the one who has the plan and purpose for your life. Many well-meaning, God-fearing people, have gone astray, burned out, and lost their marriages based on a misplaced allegiance to their spiritual calling. The same is true in commercial settings, where people have become so obsessed with financial success that they leave their families behind and paid a big price. So I ask again: What do you want? What do you really want?

Take the time to sit down with those who are important to you and discuss the roadmap for your life. The priorities that you have and the allocation of resources, including time and focus, are all important factors that need to be taken into account when you are setting the direction and passion for your life.

May I give you a small example from my own life? I am often asked to speak and to contribute and serve on boards. Deciding beforehand what time is available to serve and how much speaking or writing I will do is important. If I did not put in place a plan and structure, I could quite easily become overcommitted and therefore unable to give my best.

With directorships, for example, I have decided to have one commercial, two not-for-profit, and one industry or leadership board. I believe this maximizes my contribution. It also meets some of my career aspirations and ensures that I have time not only to serve with excellence in these capacities but also not to get too committed and therefore risk damaging other aspects of my life.

While you are thinking about priorities, it is important to look at the various ministries you are involved in. If you have a wife or husband, you have a ministry to serve him or her, cherish him or her, spend time with him or her, support him or her, encourage him or her, and minister to him or her.

If you have children, likewise this responsibility is a ministry before God. Your ministry in the workplace is obviously important—maybe more than you realize—and hopefully as you finish reading this book, you will see that it is a true ministry and a true calling. We are also called to serve in the local church and be a part of the community and contribute to that area of our collective lives.

There may be other things you are involved in—other areas you are passionate about, other God-given desires in your heart to help and to serve. God says He'll give us the desires of our hearts (Ps. 37:4). Often they are there because He places them within us. Just as He has made us unique, we also have a unique place in life to fill. That requires a unique set of talents and abilities.

Given these competing areas of our lives, it is often hard to set priorities. Listing things in order of most importance is often quite difficult. Priorities, when set, don't necessarily mean exclusion of one thing rather than another. They can often be all included but each set at a different pace. Your part-time passion for a particular hobby may take a while to develop over a period of time given only a short allocation of available time.

Your ministry at work may become a larger priority because you believe it is God ordained and an important part of your life. Getting this structure right is quite important. Despite needing constant readjustment due to different demands at different times, a clear roadmap and allocation of time is important. The allocation should be proportionate to the priority.

When I tried to adopt this framework into my life, it meant letting go of a lot of things. But I have found that it has meant that I was much more effective in areas that are important. Understanding God's priorities and His will is a prerequisite to establishing a balanced life. If you are not sure how to hear from God, we will cover that a little later. When in doubt, and if you are not sure what He is saying, use your best judgment and allow Him to correct and recalibrate as necessary.

All these things are interconnected. The most productive people I've had working for me are those with strong relationships and interests outside of work and who don't work excessive hours. The fallacy of long hours equaling high productivity is long gone.

In business it is always important to have a clear strategy. This is always linked to a clear vision. The vision is a position in the future you wish to attain. As it is with business, so it should be with our lives in general.

Personally, I apply the same process. I have a three-year view and a one-year view, both based on ten key milestones. These reflect all different areas of my life. From family to business, all aspects are catered for, and their priorities are borne out in the rate of change or the sequence and elevation of goals.

These ten, one-year milestones are then broken down to 90-day steps—just the next 90 days. So much can change so quickly that it is important in life as well as in business, of course, to ensure that our strategic direction is available for review. However, a structured strategy of key milestones with clear, demonstrable, and measurable goals written down, with some accountability attached, can ensure a direction that is balanced, effective, and productive.

Boundaries

One of the hardest things to do, but an important skill to learn, is how to say no. There is something in us that wants to say yes and that doesn't want to offend. This is a good trait. However, it can also cause a lot of trouble. Here is a little pearl of wisdom for you. I can't remember where I heard it, but I adopted it immediately: "A need doesn't constitute a call." Just because there is something that needs to be done doesn't necessarily mean you are the one who needs to do it. Often when you say yes, you may well cause someone else who is meant to step up from receiving a blessing due to him or her. Often people will stand aside, assuming that you will do something. When you don't, others will be released into their ministries.

If you are aware of your limitations, are aware of your priorities, have committed to a strategy, and have a structure in place to allocate your resources, including your time, then you can politely say no in confidence, knowing that it is the best for you, your family, and those you are ministering to in your various areas of influence. As Matthew 5:37 says, *"Simply let your 'Yes' be 'Yes' and your 'No' 'No'"* (NIV1984).

Have a clear vision, a clear purpose, a clear strategy, and a clear structure and see your life blossom in the areas that God has anointed you to minister. Saying no merely protects what you have established and will continue to enable you to be fruitful.

Talents

Every talent we have comes from God. We are unique, and we have a unique niche to fill. No one else can do what we do, bring what we bring, and have the impact we have. This is why being ourselves is key to success. Let there be no masks, and always be authentic. As leaders it is okay to be vulnerable, authentic, and real. We are most effective when we are genuine.

We are individually positioned to have a unique impact. Our makeup, our personalities, and all that we have that differentiates us from others is what will make us successful in what God has called us to do. The closer we can be, to the person we are, to whom God has made us to be, the more effective, productive, and satisfied we will be.

We may spend a lot of time looking at other people and wanting to have their talents. There is an attitude in each one of us that desires to be something different or that perhaps envies the gifts and talents given to another. In reality, we should be embracing who God has made us to be. In this mindset is the foundation of full satisfaction. In this perspective is contentment, because being all we want to be is found in being all we can be. Being who you are and allowing God to show and to mold you into being the best you can be is the empowered life, the God-given life, and is truly living life to fulfill your God-given purpose.

Patience

One of the lessons learned through challenge and difficulties in a work environment is patience. Give me patience, and give it to me right now. Galatians 5:22 tells us that patience is a fruit of the Holy Spirit: *"But the fruit of the Spirit is love, joy, peace, forbearance, kindness, goodness, faithfulness."*

So how is this imparted into our lives? I believe it comes with Him as He is in us. But to be fully manifest in us, it has to be exercised. This is true of all the fruits of the Spirit. They all can be developed as we yield ourselves to Him in the workplace. Fruit on a tree only comes with maturity, but gifts can be placed on an immature tree. It is by their fruit we are to judge people. As Matthew 7:17 says, *"Likewise, every good tree bears good fruit, but a bad tree bears bad fruit."* We will build patience, perseverance, and faith as we face and overcome trials, but we need to recognize the opportunity and the fellowship of the Holy Spirit as He challenges and changes us.

"Is it not from the mouth of the Most High that both calamities and good things come?" (LAM 3:38).

Here is another word about hard times from God. I am not sure I want to hear that. Surely a loving Father would not allow such things to happen. Yet His ways are not our ways, and His thoughts are not our thoughts. He has eternal things in mind, and we all too easily focus on the temporal.

Our surrender to God is not only an invitation for Him to come in but also a willingness to let Him be Lord here and now, in the good and the bad. But let us not forget the life after this one—a future with Him, a heaven to gain and a hell to avoid. His free gift is eternal life, but it cost Him His Son. His love for us is intimate and infinite; it is in the hard times that we truly learn to trust.

Perseverance

One outcome from a disciplined life, from spending time with God in prayer, and from reading His Word will be an ability to persevere. This goes beyond our normal human understanding. This is a divine perseverance, an ability to endure, and a capacity to break through in the power of the Holy Spirit.

The modern workplace has many demands as we seek to find balance and blend our complex and busy lives. Priorities have to be set and boundaries placed when health, fitness, family, friends, and time with God all compete with a busy work schedule. Yet we are asked to work heartily in Colossians 3:23: *"Whatever may be your task, work at it heartily (from the soul), as [something done] for the Lord and not for men."*

Often perseverance is not enduring a fiery trial. It can be dealing with the mundane, the simple, and the day-to-day drudgery that sometimes weighs us down. What carries you through the dull and mundane? We all have those tasks we don't look forward to—the ones we tend to avoid. Yet there is a higher way where we recognize the value of serving God in the insignificant.

It is something we need to cognitively acknowledge. We also need to shift our hearts and spirits to recognize the manifest presence of God in the simplest tasks done with love. I think our true faith is manifest and evidenced in the mundane, not in the spectacular.

Glory to Glory

It stands to reason that Jesus was the most-effective Christian there has ever been. That sounds like an odd statement. In a way it is, yet it is nonetheless true. He is the full embodiment of everything it is to serve and follow God. He was fully God, yes, but He was also fully man. He demonstrated how to follow God. He did nothing out of His own divinity but only operated under the unction and power of the Holy Spirit. He only did what He saw His father doing.

"Jesus gave them this answer: 'I tell you the truth, the Son can do nothing by himself; he can do only what he sees his Father doing, because whatever the Father does the Son also does'" (JOH 5:19 NIV1984).

And so it is with us. We need to rely on the empowerment of the Holy Spirit and the guidance of the Father to be effective in what God has called us to do at work.

Part of our walk with God is that He will endeavor to change us to become more like Jesus. If you're anything like me, the very thought is staggering and unfathomable. The closer I get to God, the more I realize how far I am from Him. Yet to be effective in His kingdom—to be truly effective—we need to allow the Holy Spirit to train us, change us, and transform us into His image. This is not a denial of who we are but a way to allow God to make us into all we can be.

We have covered the fundamentals of laying a foundation so we are available to be changed and so God will use our work to shape and mold us. But it is the direction of His desired destination that is truly staggering.

"And we, who with unveiled faces all reflect the Lord's glory, are being transformed into his likeness with ever-increasing glory, which comes from the Lord, who is the Spirit" (2 COR 3:18 NIV1984).

We are being changed from glory to glory into the image of Jesus Christ. We have a long way to go. Well, I can only speak for myself; you may well be a long way down the track. He is changing us from glory to glory into His image as we respond in faith to what He is doing and asking us to do. We need to learn to hear and heed that still, quiet voice, the gentle promptings of the Holy Spirit.

It is often said that God is a gentleman, one who will only go where we allow Him to, where we freely give up areas of our lives to His influence. This is wholly true, yet I have found Him sometimes pounding on the walls and putting me in circumstances, where I really have no choice but to yield. I count that a privilege. Sometimes we are slow to yield and have little understanding of God's full desire for the purposes of our lives.

We have yet to see what God could do with a man who is fully yielded to the Spirit. One thing is for sure though: God uses the workplace to shape, mold, and form us into the best we can be and to unlock our potential. The manifestation of His fruit is created as we exercise them in submission to His will and purposes. It's time to get with the program, to yield our lives to God, to become effective in all He is called us to do, and to be about our Father's business at our business.

Key Scripture

> *"And we, who with unveiled faces all reflect the Lord's glory, are being transformed into his likeness with ever-increasing glory, which comes from the Lord, who is the Spirit"* (2 COR 3:18 NIV1984).

Main Points

- God uses work to shape us into His image.
- God's main concern is character, not prosperity.
- Disciplines are the foundation of growth.
- There is favor in surrender
- Pressure produces patience and perseverance.

Prayer

Lord, I am Yours, available to You; change me into Your image. Amen.

Notes

CHAPTER 4

WORK TO SERVE

"Because anyone who serves Christ in this way is pleasing to God and receives human approval"

(ROM 14:18).

The ultimate example of service has to be Jesus. He came to serve and not to be served. He demonstrated a life of sacrifice, and true, undeniable service. There is no higher calling than to do what Jesus did and serve. This is best expressed in His willingness to leave His divinity aside and to serve mankind as a man.

"Let this mind be in you which was also in Christ Jesus, who, being in the form of God, did not consider it robbery to be equal with God, but made Himself of no reputation, taking the form of a bondservant, and coming in the likeness of men" (Phi 2:5–7 NKJV).

You can have all of the capability and even the gifting, but if you do not learn to serve, you will ultimately fail. You will damage either yourself or those you lead and probably both. Longevity comes from character, and character is birthed in servant hood and the intimacy of following Jesus closely. So what does that look like in the cold, hard, commercial environment we work in? It certainly is a contrast to the status quo. Paul describes it like this in Philippians 2:3–4:*"Let nothing be done through selfish ambition or conceit, but in lowliness of mind let each esteem others better than himself. Let each of you look out not only for his own interests, but also for the interests of others"* (NKJV).

There is a lifetime of learning in that one simple but life-changing verse. We are all tempted by conceit, edifying self-image, and self-preservation. That is not the life we are called to, but it is only God who can change our hearts to better reflect His own.

But let us not confuse service and humility with being a doormat. We have watered down the concept of meekness. We have swapped meekness for weakness. Meekness is choosing to serve from a position of strength. It is a self-contained, God-ordained place of power.

So what does it mean to serve? Often when we hear the word serve, we think of denigrating our own position. In order to serve well, we need to understand who we are in Christ. Yes, it is not all about us. It is not all about me. However, we do well to operate from the foundation of sound self-esteem.

Once we fully understand that we are loved, honored, and infinitely valuable to the Father, we can rest in His assurance and recognize our value in Him. It is out of this position that we can truly serve—not out of the need to be wanted or some sense of duty but out of the appreciation of His love and of what has been given to us.

Leadership

The concept of servant leadership has been around for many years. Again, Jesus is the ultimate example of a servant leader. With leadership comes responsibility. Leadership is not given so we can lord it over those under our authority.

Leadership is about serving. It is about creating a vision, environment, and culture that will allow those around us to develop, grow, and be all they can be. Releasing people into their God-given place in life, where they can operate with the best use of their talents, is the ultimate in servant leadership.

We all have a measure of influence. We all have areas in our lives where we lead. John Maxwell in his book *The 360 Degree Leader* very aptly explains how you can be in a position to lead regardless of your position in an organization. Often the true leaders in an organization may not have the corner office and the fancy title. They are more usually those who have informal influence and personal power rather than positional power.

Faithful

We are called to be faithful whether we are leaders or not. Faithfulness sounds like a quaint, ancient trait, yet it is a definitive characteristic of great leadership. It is demonstrated in a leadership style where people come first, where they are honored, and where they are respected.

Faithfulness is being there when others run away. It believes before seeing. It hopes where there is no hope, trusting when circumstances don't look good and believing in a wonderful Savior and the God of the breakthrough.

When we hear about serving, it is often confused with weakness, just as gentleness is very rarely used as a leadership trait. Gentleness is often again related to weakness. True gentleness is not weakness but comes from a grounding of respect and honor. It comes from an understanding that knows that shouting, jumping up and down, and being unnecessarily harsh is not an effective way of motivating people.

"Servants, be submissive to your masters with all fear, not only to the good and gentle, but also to the harsh" (1 PET 2:18 NKJV).

We have all at some time had to report to someone who was harsh. Maybe it was a shareholder, director, manager, financier, supplier, or customer. In the midst of our stakeholders and authority figures, there will be some harshness. We can't get away from it; it is a part of business life and life in general, for that matter.

What should be our response when we find ourselves in this situation? Submission. That is not a popular word or concept in today's society. However, the Scripture is quite clear. Maybe it is our pride that stops us, or perhaps it is a lack of full understanding of the definition of the word. We are not called to be a doormat. Jesus was never a doormat, but He operated with a submissive stance and a willingness to serve despite how it was received or perceived. We should also operate in this way. It is a tough call, but this is God's way. He will be with us all the way, every day, equipping us when we have nothing to give.

It's easy to serve the good, but in God's program of character development, sometimes we need to serve the harsh, the ungrateful, and those we do not respect. It takes a change of heart to submit and be faithful and to serve where we have been placed.

We need to understand that God's ways are not our ways. In order to be effective in the kingdom of God, we have to learn to serve, and not out of a sense of obligation but out of a willing heart, that God's will be done, not ours.

Authentic

The biggest mistake we make in business, in our careers, and in the workplace is the false notion that we need to be or act in a particular way to be successful. The truth is, if we are in God's plan and purposes, the best we can be will always be natural, genuine, and authentic.

We are called to be ourselves. God has called us to be us—you to be you and me to be me. The closer we are to whom He made us, the more effective we will be. He has given us specific talents. We are unique, and we have a unique place. No one else can do what we do, bring what we bring, or have the impact we have. This is why being ourselves is the key to success. We should be authentic, with no masks.

As leaders it is okay to be vulnerable, to be genuinely authentic. It is okay to be wrong and to allow team accountability, transparency, and empowerment. From a leader's perspective, these attributes are evidence of a servant's heart. Releasing a team to be trusted, enabled, and equipped to achieve the task set for them is a demonstration of mature servant leadership. The basis of this will always be authenticity and a willingness to serve.

A part of serving and a key leadership characteristic, in my view, is transparency. Healthy leaders demonstrate trust and empower people to unlock their potential. If we do not allow people access to all the information required to make the decisions they need to make, it follows that we cannot empower them.

Transparency is not only about availability of information; it is also about openness to emotions. The sense of vulnerability that comes with a willingness to be open can be seen as a weakness. However, I have found it to be universally true that open dialogue and a willingness to be vulnerable engenders such a level of trust and alignment that the downside risk disappears. When we try to be someone we are not, it is always obvious to those around us. When we open up and are willing to engage fully, there is a level of understanding and authenticity that draws those around us into a true team.

"No longer do I call you slaves, for the slave does not know what his master is doing; but I have called you friends, for all things I have heard from My Father I have made known to you" (JOH 15:15 NASB).

Are openness and transparency questions of culture and leadership style, or do they carry spiritual weight? Here we see Jesus clearly demonstrating transparency, trust, and a close relationship with those He led. Control is often an illusion. Those who are too controlling move people from commitment to mere compliance and often to passive if not overt resistance.

Openness, transparency, and free communication come with a set of risks that are far outweighed by the trust and positive productivity they engender. Engagement to a clear vision and open communication are a powerful cultural mix.

Innovation, creativity, customer service, and productivity are all increased in an environment of trust and empowerment. If people don't know what's going on, they will make it up anyway; they might as well talk about what is really happening. This level of transparency has to be initiated from the top. It is the leadership style that will ultimately drive corporate behaviors.

When we think about business, and business people in particular, we often think about hard-nosed and tough individuals. There is no doubt that the commercial environment can be tough. It can be harsh and cutthroat. However, you can be willing to make tough decisions and hard calls while still remaining pleasant and operating with a servant's heart. As Proverbs 15:1 says, *"A gentle answer turns away wrath, but a harsh word stirs up anger."*

When we are in a position of authority in our company, there is a temptation to be harsh. We can easily display emotions that are not appropriate. This is especially true when faced with an angry person. The wisdom of this Scripture is that an unexpectedly gentle response can disarm a potentially volatile situation. Often when challenged we may assume a gentle answer is a sign of weakness and that authority demands a certain demeanor. This Scripture indicates a better way.

Often it is not what has to be done but how it is done that is the ultimate evidence of a servant's heart. Being pleasant, easy to deal with, and reasonable will ensure a better business result than being tough, hard-nosed, and unreasonable. Long-term relationships are what great businesses thrive on. They are based on mutual respect, honor, and being pleasant and reasonable.

Serving the vision

Creating a vision should always be a collective process. However, carrying the vision and living the vision need to be demonstrated at the leadership level. There is nothing worse than a leader who does not live the vision.

Serving the vision is the prerogative of all those who work in the business. It becomes the unbiased arbiter of direction. It becomes the impersonal but all-powerful direction for the company. Decisions made and priorities set should be aligned with the vision.

Serving the vision becomes a clarion call to serve each other in completing that vision. If you want to engender empowerment, and all good leaders do, then you need to have a clear vision. When you couple that with a servant-oriented environment, you unlock the potential of your people and therefore the business. A key part of leadership is demonstrating and constantly communicating vision—not vision as in foresight but vision as in a clearly articulated picture of the desired future state.

"Then the Lord answered me and said, 'Record the vision and inscribe it on tablets, that the one who reads it may run'" (HAB 2:2 NASB).

Without a clear vision, your team will be disparate, pulling in many directions. With a clear vision, unity will prevail. Effort will be concentrated on a desired, jointly agreed future. All levels of your business can benefit from understanding where you want to go. True servant leadership releases people with empowerment, but without a clear vision, that is not possible. Unless we all know where we are going, we can't do our piece to get there. Jesus gave a clear vision statement just before He left.

"Therefore go and make disciples of all nations…" (MAT 28:19).

That is what we are all about. After Jesus said this, He empowered us with that mandate and resourced us with the ultimate helper, the Holy Spirit. Surely we should emulate this model in our businesses.

Integrity

One key aspect of serving, and of a servant's heart, is operating in integrity. This seems like a basic, common, and well-understood requirement. However, in reality it is, like common sense, unfortunately not all that common. You cannot serve without integrity.

Do you ever feel like you are being tested? Are you going to do the right thing? What about that thing that just popped into your head? You know, the one where you know what you should really be doing but are reluctant to do? First Chronicles 29:17 says, *"I know, my God, that you test the heart and are pleased with integrity…"*

Do the right thing, and let God sort out what happens next. Integrity counts. Serving with integrity is not easy. In fact, it is quite hard. In reality it is impossible. Yet with God, all things are possible. We should not look to our own resources to operate in integrity. It is only in God that we find the true power, strength, and purity to operate with a high level of integrity.

A life of quiet, understated, yet resolute integrity is a powerful witness and an inducer of respect. Operating out of high integrity, while not being proud of our humility, will gain favor with both man and God. Doing things God's way doesn't necessarily put us at odds with those around us. Sometimes we assume that we will be less successful if we act in accordance to Scripture.

"For He who serves God in these things is acceptable to men and approved by God" (ROM 14:18).

I would take having favor with God over favor with man, but God says you can achieve both. Just make sure you get the priority right. One is the cause and the other the effect. This Scripture tells us that we can be acceptable to men and approved by God. What a powerful way to be effective in the marketplace.

Our integrity is often demonstrated by what we say. Do we offer more than we can deliver? Did I paint a picture that is overly rosy? Did you offer an incentive in front of your staff that will be impossible to meet?

Sometimes it is not easy to say it like it is. Often when circumstances change, we struggle to meet our commitments. Perhaps we should do what we said we will do and let God sort out the consequences. He will honor a stand that is done in line with His requirements of us.

We can live by the Word of God and keep our promises and run or be any part of a successful, growing, profitable, influential business. There is something elegant, honest, and pure about simplicity. Keep it simple.

Sometimes it is the simple things that trip us up. Trust Jesus to set the standard, to make it simple, and to tell it like it is. He has a way of stating the obvious in such a simple way that it becomes profound beyond all reason.

What is His idea of integrity and statement of honesty? Simply put, He said in Matthew 5:37, *"But let your 'Yes' be 'Yes,' and your 'No,' 'No...'"* There is power in simple truth—just walking in simple integrity, doing what we say. How often do we increase complexity in our answers or try to manipulate with a little white lie?

How would others view us if they believed we would always give a straight answer, with no hidden agendas, just the truth? If we walked in that way, it would be counter to usual behavior. Wouldn't you want to work and do business with someone like that? Then, when we shared something about God, maybe they would believe that as well.

Serving with honesty

One of my favorite characters in the Bible is Daniel. He was placed in a set of circumstances most of us could not imagine. He was taken from his home as a slave and put in the palace of a brutal heathen king. When was the last time you were thrown to the lions? Daniel demonstrated a life committed to God that we should all aspire to. He was hardworking, trustworthy, and full of wisdom. When people stood against Daniel, they could find nothing that would discredit him. What a wonderful testimony.

"At this, the administrators and the satraps tried to find grounds for charges against Daniel in his conduct of government affairs, but they were unable to do so. They could find no corruption in him, because he was trustworthy and neither corrupt nor negligent" (Dan 6:4 NIV1984).

Can we be measured in the same way and not be found wanting? I find that to be quite a challenge. Daniel's life is one that I will consistently try to emulate. If we do this, our honesty can testify for us, and we like Daniel, will be trusted with much more.

"And my honesty will testify for me in the future, whenever you check on the wages you have paid me" (Gen 30:33 NIV1984).

Quality

We have concentrated so far on serving inside our businesses. While this is key and often a catalyst for success, obviously we cannot forget about our customers. Serving them is paramount for success in any commercial venture. Many businesses have come unstuck when they have failed to honor, respect, and serve their customers. We live in a global environment, with information and availability of resources like never before. Our people, and how we serve our customers, will ultimately be our true sustainable point of difference.

Service is often seen as a cost center. In my view, it is an opportunity center. Many great clients have been born out of a problem that has been well solved. What does your company do when the wheels fall off? Often our businesses are not judged by what we do when things go well but by what we do when things don't.

We are judged on our word. When the promises we make still hold water when it is not to our immediate advantage, trust is engendered. The quality of our service, both within and outside of our company, will ultimately shape our destiny.

Quality and service are equally important in product development. Providing a quality product is serving our customers. When we serve our customers well, we will get more business. It is a simple philosophy but one that has served many companies well.

This principle is true in many aspects of any company. We all serve somebody, we all have an area of influence, and we are all accountable to somebody. Why not take the time to do a quality job, to produce a quality service, or to create a quality product?

Consistency is evidence of planning, thought, anticipation, and integrity in delivery. This is about reliability, a constant delivery of quality, anticipation of issues and problems, and overcoming them regardless of the circumstances. Consistency is evidence of a business that knows what it's doing, and what is true of the business is true of the individual.

Can people rely on us? When we are asked to do something, do people have confidence that we will deliver what we say? These are challenging questions, but they are ones that need to be asked. Consistency does sound dull, yet it is a demonstration of commitment and a great trait to have. It definitely engenders trust and is part of serving well with quality.

Inspiration

What do inspiration and serving have in common? Certainly the desire to serve needs to be born out of thankfulness to God. True inspiration, by definition, comes from Him. Part of serving God and serving those around us in the marketplace needs to come from a place of inspiration.

Product development and service can be inspired. There are always ways we can serve better, ideas that are born in the heart of God, and truly inspirational thoughts that will impact our business that are available to us as we seek Him.

God is the creator and the origin of all creative thought; He created the creation. What if we had access to the smartest people on the planet? Would we not take advantage of the personal relationships we had? Would we not ask what they thought or use their expertise to help drive excellence in our own businesses? Yet we have a resource that is infinitely greater, infinitely smarter, and available to us every day.

Serving those around us, those we influence, and those in authority over us is an important part of what is to be a Christian in the marketplace. One aspect of that service is bringing access to God to bear in a workplace.

We are channels of inspiration connected to the Creator. Surely that means we should be very effective. Often we do not have because we do not ask. Taking business issues to God and waiting on Him for an answer should be a daily part of what we do, who we are, and how we serve.

Let's not squander the authority and relationship we have but rather unlock the potential that has been given to us to impact our business, the workplace, and the broader marketplace. Who knows what could happen with the right idea and a servant's heart?

We are plugged into the One Who is all knowing, has all knowledge, and is all understanding. He not only understands us today but also sees the future in full clarity. Not even the smartest of us do that. What an opportunity to see and serve.

I don't know about you, but I could do with more understanding—in particular the understanding that comes from the revelation of the Holy Spirit. He is waiting to be invited into your business and wants to walk with you, guiding, leading, empowering, and bringing understanding as you seek to serve.

"The fear of the Lord is the beginning of wisdom, and knowledge of the Holy One is understanding" (PRO 9:10).

Let's not relegate God's wisdom and our understanding to a seemingly sacred context. Being vitally interested in our vocation, our calling at work, He is always willing to give insight. Why not invite Him into your business world again today?

Innovation

We have a relationship with God, the great Creator, so surely we should be the most innovative people on earth. Many of history's great breakthroughs in art, science, politics, and even democratic capitalism were born of men and women who served God. If it was true then and God is the same yesterday, today, and forever, then it is true today.

We can serve by being innovative. We add value to those around us, the project and products we produce, the services we render, and the influence we have. Those in authority over us, the ones to whom we are accountable, should recognize us as innovative.

Innovation does not just pertain to physical product ideas. We can also be innovative in the way we serve, the way we relate to people, and the respect and honor we show all those in the workplace.

If we understand that God is interested in our work, then let's put that into practice and ask Him to show us ways to improve our businesses and workplaces. Regardless of whatever position we find ourselves in, there is an opportunity to seek God and produce fruit, in keeping with the kingdom. As we surrender our lives to Him, we can expect Him to move on our behalf and begin to show up in our daily work.

Attitude

What should our attitude be as we serve in the workplace? Should it be one of grudging obligation—one where we miserably serve, downtrodden, woe is me, here I am forced to serve you yet again? I'm sure there would be lines of people wanting to become Christians if we had that attitude. Our attitude impacts our effectiveness. Although the positive thinking brigade has hijacked this truth, it is nonetheless a truth we would do well to heed.

As a man thinks in his heart, so he is. Attitude is always a choice. It is one of the few things we actually have full control over. The attitude we choose will often determine the outcome of our day and the effectiveness of what we are engaged in. As the cliché says, our attitude determines our altitude. It is a cliché, but it is only a cliché because it is true. As Proverbs 18:21 says, *"The tongue has the power of life and death, and those who love it will eat its fruit"* (PRO 18:21).

"A good man brings good things out of the good stored up in his heart, and an evil man brings evil things out of the evil stored up in his heart. For the mouth speaks what the heart is full of" (LUK 6:45).

Our heart is influenced by what we say and by the attitude we adopt. If we choose to have a positive outlook and to trust God, then this can give us a heart of peace. Then the words we say will be uplifting, generous, encouraging, and positive. We will then be enabled to impact our environment for good and not allow circumstances to stand in the way of establishing the kingdom of God.

The faithful stance of standing on the Word of God and trusting in His promises is an outworking of an appropriate attitude. If we are negative and focus on circumstances, then the words that come from our lips will not be ones of faith, and they will not agree with what God has said. This literality impacts the circumstances and situations in which we find ourselves.

The power of positive confession—of agreeing with God's view and promises—will impact our circumstances for good. We will see the fulfillment of God's will, but it starts with the right attitude. Faith cannot be conjured up by the will, but we can create an environment where faith prospers. The seed of faith is cultivated in the right environment if we choose an attitude that is in line with God's will.

Imagine if there were an army of people who came to work with an expectation that God would impact of their day. They would turn up motivated, empowered, and expecting the best and would serve with integrity, inspired by God. We would turn the world upside down in very short time.

Motivation

What is it that motivates you? Many things motivate me—everything from financial gain to recognition to overcoming a challenge to creating a great environment to releasing people into their God-given destinies. But there is one motivation that should be above all others for those of us who serve God. Those last two words say it all: 'serve God.'

It is Jesus Who we serve in a workplace. He should be the motivation for us to serve. He demonstrated what was to serve by taking off His robe, fastening a towel around His waist, and washing the hands and feet of those who would betray and deny Him in a few short days' time.

Jesus demonstrated the ultimate motivation in coming to seek those who were lost and to honor His Father by being obedient to Him even unto death on the cross. That is our motivation and our model: to serve God like Jesus did.

Motivation should drive us to be diligent and to exercise the skills we have to serve those in authority over us, those around us, and those we have been given authority over. We should treat all those different parties with the same respect and honor.

We also need to serve ourselves. Serving is not as selfless as it sounds. The more we develop our own skills, the gifts and talents we have been given, and the attitudes God has placed in us, the more able we are to serve others.

"Be diligent to present yourself approved to God, a worker who does not need to be ashamed" (2 Tim 2:15 NKJV).

Those in leadership can be very susceptible to this. Do not neglect what God has given to you. The sharper we keep ourselves, the more effective we will be.

How is your skill level? Have you, like a lot of leaders, neglected your own development to serve your company? Diligence is not only applying yourself to your duties with vigor; it is also ensuring you are advancing and growing.

If you look after yourself, you will often have more to give others. Do not neglect reading, learning, listening to wisdom, and attending a seminar or meeting together with like-minded businesspeople. Be diligent in your own growth and development and those around you will benefit. Then you will be able to present yourself to God as a worker who does not need to be ashamed.

In the midst of our servitude, let's be wholehearted. We should be able to serve with joy. As we work wholeheartedly, fully engaged in what we're doing and with the right motivation and attitude, we will succeed.

"In everything that he undertook in the service of God's temple and in obedience to the law and the commands, he sought his God and worked wholeheartedly. And so he prospered" (2 Chr 31:21).

Unfortunately we can't talk about being a servant without talking about humility. This may seem to contrast against a motivation, but if our motivation is to serve, we need to operate in humility. We seem to have traditionally lumped humility in with meekness and mildness. We need to get away from the modern way Jesus is pictured and portrayed. He is emasculated, meek and mild, and painted with effeminate features in a white robe, with clean feet.

This is very different from a rugged carpenter having a solid, real, and tangible rough, tough life. Just as meekness is centered in strength, so humility is centered in an awareness of who we are in Him.

Humility is not putting yourself down. It is raising others up. Humility understands that we are seated at the right hand of the father in Christ. When He looks at us, He sees the righteousness of Jesus. Humility understands that this is not from us or anything we can do but is a gift from God.

The greatness we are called to is manifest in humility and servant hood. As Matthew 23:11 says, *"The greatest among you will be your servant."* This paradoxical truth is perfectly presented in the person of Jesus. The greatest of all was the servant of all. As we seek to serve others, God will exalt us. As we seek to be exulted, He may well oppose the proud. This is counter to human nature because we all want significance and to be esteemed.

There is a part of us that will tend to use others to advance ourselves. We need to be reminded of God's way to counter our own ambition. We need to redefine things we have seen as weaknesses and allow them to become strengths in our lives as we serve God. Let's learn from the Master and learn to serve.

Key Scripture

> *"For he who serves God in these things is acceptable to God and approved by men"* (ROM 14:18 NKJV).

Main Points

- Serving others at work is serving God.
- Real leaders are faithful, transparent, and authentic.
- We are called to serve with integrity and honesty.
- Inspiration and innovation are God marks.
- Our attitude determines our effectiveness.
- Be motivated with humility.

Prayer

Teach me to serve, Lord, and keep me humble as I see You move on my behalf. Amen.

Notes

CHAPTER 5
WORK TO WITNESS

"But you shall receive power (ability, efficiency, and might) when the Holy Spirit has come upon you, and you shall be My witnesses in Jerusalem and all Judea and Samaria and to the ends (the very bounds) of the earth"

(ACTS 1:8 AMP).

If we were to purely look at things from an eternal perspective, then only those things with an eternal consequence are relevant and important. We serve an eternal God, with no beginning and no end. The last instructions Jesus left us when He was here on earth were to go into the entire world and make disciples of all people.

We have been born again not only because of the conviction of our sin by the Holy Spirit but because somebody was obedient and had the conviction and courage to take a chance and tell us about Jesus. I did not hear the reason for Jesus' death and resurrection until I was 19 years old. We assume that people know, and they just don't.

The consequences of going to eternity without Christ are too horrific to contemplate and realize fully. If we truly understood the consequences, we would overcome our natural reluctance to share our faith. There is a lot at stake. We have been saved from a Christ-less eternity. When we believed in our hearts and confessed with our mouths that Jesus Christ was Lord, acknowledged our sins, and invited Him into our lives, we were born again.

"If you confess with your mouth, 'Jesus is Lord,' and believe in your heart that God raised him from the dead, you will be saved" (ROM 10:9).

We were instantly translated from the kingdom of darkness into the kingdom of light. We moved from a place of judgment and condemnation to one of forgiveness, righteousness, and peace. We received the sacrifice that Jesus made for all men.

"For all have sinned and fall short of the glory of God" (ROM 3:23).

We all need His forgiveness. It is a free gift so that none may boast. It has nothing to do with works, rank, or privilege. It's just grace, pure and simple—nothing more. We have the answer for the question of eternity. The good news has been entrusted to us, and we have a responsibility and a duty to share with those who are lost, that they may have the opportunity to know our loving heavenly Father and share in eternity with Christ.

Witness is more than just a verbal confession of our faith. We can't hassle people into the kingdom because it is the Holy Spirit Who does the convicting. We are called to be witnesses not only with our mouths but also with our deeds, for faith without works is dead. We are to witness by the way we live, and it should be obvious to all Who we serve.

"Always be prepared to give an answer to everyone who asks you to give the reason for the hope that you have. But do this with gentleness and respect" (1 PET 3:15).

So how does this work out in the modern marketplace? Do we bring our four-kilo Bible to work and start bashing people with it? That will probably succeed in inoculating people against Christianity. I think there is a fundamental error that has been made in workplace evangelism. That is that we work so we can evangelize. Another way this view is manifest is that we have friendships so we can evangelize.

While any Christian who has a revelation of eternal judgment and received the wonderful gift of salvation will clearly have a heart to see people saved, it is an outcome of who we are, not an artificial construct. What I mean by that is, if you make friends to evangelize, your friendship will always be false. However, if you make friends and then share your faith, it is more likely to be authentic, real, and accepted.

As it is with friendship, so it is with work. If your sole view of why you work is to win souls, then you will never fully engage in the workplace, you won't be a part of the vision, you won't be as productive as you could be, and your efforts to engage will be contrived and artificial. Conversely, if you fully engage in the marketplace, there will be opportunities to share your faith and to see souls won for Christ.

Evangelism

I have a friend who is an extremely effective soul winner. He seems to forever be telling me of someone else who has come to know the Lord. He bumps into people on the bus, and they immediately repent and give their lives to God. Not only does he see many come to know Jesus, but he also sees them discipled and trained to become effective in their own right.

One day I made the mistake of calling him an evangelist. I got quite a stern reply, one that, on reflection, showed a lot of truth. He insisted he was not an evangelist, but he did say that he was deliberate about evangelism. He actually allotted time in his schedule to pray and witness and was fruitful accordingly. Because he is focused on seeing the opportunity and prayerful in seeking God for the salvation of those he works with, his life is fruitful.

This is something we need to think about on an ongoing basis. Tuning our hearts into what God is doing and who He is convicting and recognizing the opportunities He places in front of us each day has to become an intrinsic part of our walk at work.

Have you noticed something about evangelism? You cannot argue people into the kingdom of God. Intellectual reasoning may satisfy some need to rationally understand the argument. However, it is only the conviction of the Holy Spirit that can truly bring the revelation of our need for salvation.

If we rely solely on our own wisdom and effort, we will fail. We need to model Jesus and operate as He did if we want to see our lives fruitful with a harvest. Jesus said that He only did the things He saw His Father doing.

"Jesus gave them this answer: 'I tell you the truth, the Son can do nothing by himself; he can do only what he sees his Father doing, because whatever the Father does the Son also does'" (JOHN 5:19 NIV1984).

If that was good enough for Jesus, it's probably good enough for us. We need to rely on the Holy Spirit and on Him alone.

"But you shall receive power (ability, efficiency, and might) when the Holy Spirit has come upon you, and you shall be My witnesses in Jerusalem and all Judea and Samaria and to the ends (the very bounds) of the earth" (ACTS 1:8 AMP).

It is He who will give us power, ability, efficiency, and might. That is a great combination, and it's all we need to be successful in our quest to see people come to the revelation of Jesus Christ. Every knee will ultimately bow to Jesus; let's pray that more bow on this side of eternity where there is still time, mercy, and grace.

There is no doubt that we are all called to evangelism. We have the opportunity every day to see God move. There are opportunities to have divine encounters to share the gospel, and we should move in a state of expectation.

Where would we be without witness? Letting people know what has happened to us is a fundamental part of following Jesus. Why do we need to invite people to church to hear about Jesus? The Holy Spirit is the only one who convicts of sin, calls to repentance, and brings about the wonderful regeneration of our souls, as we move into communion with the Father.

It is in the world—in the marketplace—that we need to be testifying naturally, spontaneously, and under the Spirit's guidance as He gives opportunity. So often when we talk about reaching the lost, it is aimed at the poor, the needy, and those overseas. God loves the rich, wealthy, powerful, and influential just as much. We are called to be salt and light and to grow where we are planted. In the marketplace, our lives, actions, responses, and words—who we are and what we do—should demonstrate the love of God for a fallen world.

We are fallen sinners saved by grace, but we are now redeemed by God, bought for an incredible price. It behooves us to reach out to those around us and share the gift that was given so freely to us.

It is our duty to demonstrate God's love and influence the world around us for good. It is, after all, the good news.

Reputation

I cringe when I hear people who don't know Jesus commenting on what Christians are like in business. It is unfortunately true that many people who are followers of Christ fail to live out His mandate to be a witness in the marketplace. People are watching to see if our faith is genuine. Our reputation not only impacts us but also the One we profess to represent. After all, in Proverbs 22:1, God says, *"A good name is more desirable than great riches; to be esteemed is better than silver or gold."*

Avoiding shortcuts and not burning bridges are two ways of protecting your reputation. Being pleasant to deal with, regardless of how difficult a situation or how bad a deal goes, will ensure your reputation stays in place. The Bible places such things above material gain and above precious jewels. So we too should have the same perspective. We are the physical manifestation of God's love to the world, after all.

Often people will judge God by how they see us. That may be unreasonable, but it is reality. Protecting our reputation protects God's reputation. We are His representatives. Isn't that a big responsibility? Yes it is and one we should take very seriously. We are in a war for the souls, hearts, and minds of those around us.

Opportunity

If it is the Holy Spirit who convicts people of their sin and their need for Jesus, then He is the orchestrator and instigator of what needs to occur for the witness to be effective. We can accomplish little in our own strength. We need to have sensitivity to hearing from God.

When Jesus ministered to the people around Him, He did so in a multitude of ways. There is no formula, no seven steps, and no instant answer. Each case is different, and God will draw people in different ways. We need to be available to Him, and He will show us the way.

Allow me to give you an illustration from my own life. I was on a plane on the way to Hong Kong. I like flying. It is one of the few places left where you can truly be left in peace, with no phones, no email, and no meetings; a time to relax. I know this is changing, but it would be a tragedy to see phone calls and email readily available on flights.

I sat down in my seat after a busy week, looking forward to watching some of Hollywood's finest mind-numbing material. I said a brief, polite hello to the person next to me, put my headphones on, and settled into a time of blissful isolation.

I started to get a sense of discomfort, an unsettling in my spirit. I could hear that still, quiet voice somewhere deep inside me, urging me to put aside my own comfort and engage with the guy sitting next to me. I have learned over the years to respond to those promtings. Yet still, I debated in my mind whether this was God or me. In the end I relented, put down my headphones, and began to engage with my fellow traveler.

We talked a little business and a few other things and made polite conversation. But then we began to talk more about personal issues and relationships. He began to share some of his life story. He was a very wealthy man, having made a small fortune from investments. He was a mover and shaker in the Chinese banking system. It turned out he was a Buddhist, and he was gay.

What did I have in common with a rich, powerful, Chinese, gay Buddhist? Why would God place me in a situation to share His love with this man? It turned out that he had just broken up with his long-term partner. This was a time in his life when he was hurting and vulnerable. A loving God was reaching out to this hurting man. This was perhaps one of only a handful of opportunities where this man would be open and potentially receptive enough to hear about Jesus and receive truth into his spirit.

We shared some of our life stories with each other. I was able to talk about Jesus, and it changed some of his misconceptions. His view was that Christians hated gays, and he assumed God was the same. God gave me the words that would maintain relationship yet reveal His central truth, and the gospel was shared with this man for the first time in his life. God had a plan a purpose and an undying love for this gentleman.

I share this example not because it was one of a successful conversion, because it wasn't. But I share it for two reasons. First, there is no formula for this kind of encounter. You can't go to your local Christian bookshop and order the book on the seven steps to converting rich, powerful, Chinese, gay Buddhists.

Second, those we may think are a long way from God or may judge are loved by our heavenly Father. The conversations I had and the gospel I shared have sown seeds into that man's life. It was such a natural conversation, and the fact that a Christian would talk in this way to him completely shocked him. His perspective of Jesus was challenged and changed. Every time I tell this story as an illustration, I pray for him, that the seeds placed in his heart by God would germinate, grow, and eventually bear the fruit of salvation.

Being tuned in to what we see our Father in heaven doing is an important part of walking with Him. Perhaps we should bear in mind that the Holy Spirit's agenda is often different from ours and that His ways are not our ways.

Effective Model

I enter into this section with a certain amount of trepidation. That is not because I am unconvinced of its validity but because it is very counter cultural. The prevailing paradigm is being challenged by the current move of God in the marketplace.

Let me reiterate once again that I am a strong supporter of the local church. Having said that, I do not believe the church is operating in the most efficient and scriptural way. In the midst of the changes that will occur, we need to be careful that we do not divide. The marketplace movement and the local church need to work together to see the advancement of the kingdom of God. It is not the time to divide, as some are suggesting. It is not a case of 'either or' but of 'both and.'

It is an area where I think we have just gone wrong but for all the right reasons. In the current model, we try to get people to come to church. We try to convince people who don't know Christ to come into a completely foreign environment where they are uncomfortable, in unfamiliar surroundings, and in a minority and hand them over to a professional to get them saved. My Bible tells me very clearly that pastors and teachers are there to equip "the people" for "works of service." We who are in the marketplace are meant to be the ministers of the good news.

"It was He who gave some to be apostles, some to be prophets, some to be evangelists, and some to be pastors and teachers, to prepare God's people for works of service, so that the body of Christ may be built up" (EPH 4:11–12 NIV1984).

The church as an institution populated with the fivefold ministries, is to "prepare you for works of service." The church's role is to prepare the laity for the work to be done outside the church in the marketplace.

Even when this is recognized in some churches, there is a misunderstanding of what those works of service are. Often the assumption of those who equip the church is that they are a duplication of the gifts exercised by the fivefold ministers, but that is not true. If you follow that model, you will build a network of people who meet, prepare, minister, and pray but never engage in the battle, never go over the wall, and don't engage in the marketplace fulfilling their callings and operating in their true purpose, comfortable in their marketplace gifting and bearing fruit for the King.

The full expression of our work with God is to be manifested in our daily lives, not within the four walls of the church. However, it is vital to be well connected to a place of worship where you can be refreshed and prepared as you go out again to minster in the world.

We are called to be fishers of men, not keepers of the aquarium. Just imagine what would happen if we all were available and expectant to reach the lost at work. That is a much more effective and I believe biblical model. Right now we are just not getting the job done.

The witness we need and the demonstration of the grace of God, the fruit of the Spirit, and the gifts of the Spirit, in whatever way you deem them to manifest, need to be in the marketplace. Jesus very rarely ministered in the synagogue. Most of what He did, and we are to follow His example, was done wherever He was. He ministered to those around Him wherever He found them. Sometimes it was by the well, in the marketplace, by the roadside, at a party, at a wedding or a funeral—just wherever He was.

Discipleship

The last command Jesus gave us was not to make converts. He was very clear that we are to make disciples. Conversion, while it is critical for salvation, is only the first step on a long journey. Discipleship is walking alongside people until they can walk and lead others to Christ. Even then each of us needs to walk alongside, support, and encourage one another.

True discipleship is teaching people to become closer to Jesus. It is helping them discover who they are in Him, who they can be, and ensuring they have a robust and vital relationship with their Creator.

If we have had the privilege of leading someone to Christ, we have the obligation to ensure that he or she is ministered to and well discipled. We must ensure that people of maturity surround them—those who can help them grow. This enables them to be established on a firm foundation. That includes making sure they are plugged into a local community that can love them.

There is a definite witness in effective discipleship that is created by the changes that are seen in a new convert. As God begins to birth a new desire in the convert's heart, he or she will in turn encourage others to seek Him. What a privilege it is to not only see people come into the kingdom but to also see them grow, become established, and be fruitful and multiply.

Example

Our walk is our witness. We are called to be an example—an example of what it is to live an empowered life and what it means to know Jesus. "Preach the gospel at all times; when necessary, use words," is a quote commonly attributed to St. Francis of Assisi. He also preached, but this quote soundly articulates that actions do speak louder than words. We need to walk the talk. Faith without works is dead. Works without faith is equally futile.

How do you treat people? Giving people the same respect and honor Jesus would is the starting point for our witness. We should be the embodiment of what it means to be a Christian. Being Christ-like is our challenge.

Yes, we are human, and people can see our vulnerabilities, our failings, and our sin. Yet in the midst of all that, there needs to be some integrity in our walk and a definitive link between what we say and what we do. Whether we like it or not, people will judge God by what they see in us. Whilst that may be unreasonable, and in many cases unfortunate, it is nonetheless true.

Has there been a transformation in our lives that demonstrates we have had an encounter with the living God? That is a tough question that is not easy to answer because we live with our own issues and troubles. However, the truth remains that we are to be transformed, and as we allow the Holy Spirit to transform us, He will be evidenced in our lives.

There is a lot of responsibility in being an example. Yet in the midst of the pressure to unlock our potential, we can rest in the knowledge that it is God who transforms the hearts of men. It is the Holy Spirit who convicts, and He will use us if we are available and obedient.

Being an example is not about being a goody-goody. It is about being real, open, and transparent and sharing our lives with those around us. It is about a willingness to be engaged and available for the community. This willingness to be open can be threatening, but it is a necessary part of reaching out to those who need to know the love of God.

Breaking Barriers

Our God is the God of the breakthrough. If He can truly move mountains, and I know He can, then we should be the ones who break the impossible barriers—who gain the impossible deals and achieve the impossible goals. Do we believe that? Sometimes we will believe it in our minds but not in our hearts.

"He replied, 'Because you have so little faith. I tell you the truth, if you have faith as small as a mustard seed, you can say to this mountain, "Move from here to there" and it will move. Nothing will be impossible for you'" (MAT 17:20 NIV1984).

When we make a stand and put our trust in God, we should expect mountains to move. We are seated in heavenly places at the right hand of God in Christ. Authority is not based on how we feel in the morning or whether we failed yesterday. It is based on the Word of God and His promises to us. It is based on our position in Christ. We are in Him, and the authority we have, hard though it is to believe, is the authority of Jesus. When we ask in His name, it is like Him asking. What would the Father deny Jesus?

"And God raised us up with Christ and seated us with him in the heavenly realms in Christ Jesus" (EPH 2:6).

Is there something in your workplace that everybody has given up on? Is there something there that you know you can't achieve on your own? If there is, then there is an opportunity for God to demonstrate His power, His favor on you and to be glorified.

We should not shrink back from the big challenges. It is in them that we show and demonstrate that God is in the house. I will talk more about this in the next chapter, where we will explore creating with God. Meanwhile, it is enough to say that if we are achieving breakthrough, achieving the impossible, and doing things others are not capable of doing, some will ask how. There is a powerful witness in allowing God to do the impossible and for Him to get the glory.

Our Reactions

How do we react in times of success, and who gets the credit? Allocating credit can really expose the foundation on which our lives are built. If we are self-centered—and we all are to one degree or another—then we will crave the praise of men. While this is a natural tendency, choosing to give others credit for our success or at least not claiming credit as an individual rather than a team demonstrates selflessness.

In our dog-eat-dog, instant gratification world where the strongest survive and the weak are thrown away, a selfless act of attributing credit to another can be a powerful demonstration of something in you that goes beyond the individual. How we react in these circumstances can be a great witness. Do we really honor others more than ourselves? If we put them first, then that needs to be demonstrated and articulated. Watch for the opportunity to honor others; it will distinguish you from those who are self-serving. It also engenders loyalty and dedication and can move people from compliance to commitment.

While attributing success to others is not easy, taking the blame for failure is difficult. Perhaps it's only me, but I just don't like to fail. I like to succeed, but we will all fail to achieve from time to time. How do we react when this occurs? How will we react when this occurs when others are involved?

This is time for a little godly wisdom—a time to lay down our own ambition and pride and to operate with a little humility. Let God deal with the consequences if it's time to take failure on the chin. If you lead a team and you fail, then you should put your hand up to take the blame.

There is great learning and opportunities when it all goes horribly wrong. There is even a place to celebrate our most spectacular failures. It can help de-risk a culture and encourage innovation when failure is seen as an opportunity to learn and reset.

When we avoid responsibility and play the blame game, our leadership in the situation is damaged. It is again a witness that something else is going on here. It is not the normal response. It begs the questions: Why are you acting like this? Why are you willing to put your reputation on the line for us? In these circumstances, we demonstrate a behavior that shows we have a different set of priorities. We have been forgiven much.

"Therefore, I tell you, her many sins have been forgiven—for she loved much. But he who has been forgiven little loves little" (LUKE 7:47).

Those who are forgiven much love much. We know what it is to fail but also what it is to be forgiven. We know what it is like to be restored and to be loved unconditionally. We know the unreasonable, unfathomable grace and love of our heavenly Father. Blame has been shifted away from us, so who are we to blame others? Our lives should demonstrate forgiveness and humility. If we walk in these ways, people will ask why. Answering that question is the opportunity to give the glory to God and see lives touched.

It is okay to show compassion at work. It is not often that business and compassion share the same sentence. We often don't know the impact we are having. Sometimes I believe God keeps us from seeing it.

I remember going out of my way to talk with a junior staff member who had been through a personal tragedy. I didn't think much of it at the time. It was only when he brought his family in to meet me and said that I had been the only one to really care that I realized that the small gesture of compassion had had an impact. Every so often we face big problems—not the ordinary things of life but those massive, almost-overwhelming problems that rarely impact us but that can be very intimidating.

"One who is wise can go up against the city of the mighty and pull down the stronghold in which they trust" (Pro 21:22).

This is when we really need the wisdom of God. Let Him lay down the strategy, and in His strength you can overcome and pull down the mighty stronghold. Take the time to wait on Him for an answer. Often a big problem causes us immediately respond. We must be careful what we say when we are suddenly confronted with big issues. They are intended to disrupt us and place us in fear. The words we speak over the situation when we are suddenly confronted can lay a foundation for success or failure. Always speak words of faith—words that reflect God's view, not ones of failure and disaster. Life and death are in the power of what we say and how we react.

We want to act when confronted with problems because we feel doing nothing is ignoring the problem. Taking the time to hear from God can result in a suitable response empowered by Him who is the God who overcomes.

"For receiving instruction in prudent behavior, doing what is right and just and fair" (Pro 1:3).

Here is a quick checklist that should guide all our behavior and reactions in business: Is it right? Is it just? Is it fair? Often these are not considered in a business context, but if we are endeavoring to do it God's way, then this should be our reference. We get these instructions from revelation through the Word of God. Sometimes our view of what is just and fair may not be God's view, but His perspective will help us be prudent and do what is right.

Influence

We are all stewards of influence. We all have it in differing measures and in different circles. But whatever shape or form our influence takes, God gave it to us.

If we acknowledge a divine origin of our influence, it comes with some responsibility. What are we doing with it? Do we hold it lightly and with a sense of holy responsibility? Do we pray for those in our lives?

Seeing our influence as an opportunity to witness and to serve God brings our thought life and subsequent behaviors into a new realm. It is one where we are anointed to have an influence for the kingdom. Most influence is exercised through relationships. In business, they are a major key to success, whether we are dealing with those in authority over us, subordinates, peers, suppliers, customers, or any other stakeholder.

"So the craftsman encourages the smelter, and he who smooths metal with the hammer encourages him who beats the anvil" (ISA 41:7).

Suppliers are a good case in point. Are you cold and over demanding of those who supply you with goods and services? Isn't it a good business practice to extract the last possible cent from those with whom you do business? The Bible shows us a more synergistic relationship of mutual respect and encouragement.

Long-term relationships built on an understanding of shared profitability can be priceless as cycles move and pricing power shifts up and down supply and demand chains. Building those relationships on respect and going to the extent of encouraging our suppliers is doing business God's way. The very fact that it does not happen very often will ensure that you stand out, become a customer of choice, demonstrate a different approach, and represent the God you profess to serve.

I had an opportunity in one business I ran to exercise what many saw as an unreasonable act of generosity. We had great cash flow, and a lot of our suppliers were struggling during the trough in the seasonable, cyclical nature of our industry. We were ready to pay all our monthly bills, and cash flow was strong. I instructed my finance team to pay all the bills early. There was a collective convulsion from the accountants, who instantly gave me ten reasons why this was a really bad idea. The only real cost was the interest earned on the funds, which, while material, paled into insignificance against the impact that was to occur. We paid all our monthly accounts two weeks early and included a note saying we appreciated that our business was successful because of the support and service we received from our suppliers. The note also mentioned the seasonal impact our suppliers always had at this time of the year.

Needless to say, we were inundated with offers for more services and given all sorts of favor and opportunity with those we encouraged. I did have a couple of competitors ring and ask me what I thought I was doing by making them look bad. They asked me to please not make it a habit. The bottom line impact was enhanced, our reputation improved, we have favored customer status with suppliers, the industry was taking notice, and the business continued to grow and prosper.

We are stewards of influence. We all have it in different measures in different circles. God gave it to us. What are we doing with it? God will give us a measure of favor as we surrender to Him and do things His way. He has given us this influencing credibility not so we may lord it over others but so that by it we may reap a harvest as we extend the influence of the kingdom and impact our workplace for His glory.

Salt and Light

I really like the Scripture that says that we should be salt and light. There is so much truth in that short Scripture. It is one of those passages that you read again and again, and yet like the layers of an onion, it continues to reveal more and more.

"You are the salt of the earth. But if the salt loses its saltiness, how can it be made salty again? It is no longer good for anything, except to be thrown out and trampled underfoot. You are the light of the world. A town built on a hill cannot be hidden. Neither do people light a lamp and put it under a bowl. Instead they put it on its stand, and it gives light to everyone in the house. In the same way, let your light shine before others, that they may see your good deeds and glorify your Father in heaven" (MAT 5:13–16).

We are called to be like salt. We are called to operate in the physical realm just as salt does. We are called to address things that need healing or correction or to counter those things that have gone bad. Wherever we work, regardless of our position, there are opportunities to act as salt. We can quickly recognize things that are bad. The question is, what will we do about it? Are we called to ignore what we see that is wrong, or are we called to address issues as they arise? If we do choose to act, then we need wisdom in the circumstances.

The timing is almost as important as the answer. Yet if we are born of God and operating in His Spirit, we should have the confidence to address those things around us that do not match His standards. This must obviously be done in a spirit of love and not with a judgmental attitude, for Jesus did not come into the world to condemn the world, and there is no condemnation for those who are in Christ Jesus.

One of the characteristics of salt is not only its ability to heal and to cleanse but also to preserve. We carry within us an ancient wisdom handed down from generation to generation and made real in men's hearts through the Holy Spirit. We are here to preserve what is good, right, and holy. We are carriers of the truth, children of the King, and a redeemed people with a holy message that brings healing and truth.

How do we act like light? Probably the most-astounding attribute of light is that in the smallest amount, it will always expel darkness. Light a candle in the darkest room, and there is light. There is no darkness that can extinguish the smallest flame.

So it is with us. We are called to be light. Sometimes we are conned into thinking our light is insignificant. Every time we walk into work, we bring the Holy Spirit of God with us, and as He dwells in us, He will empower us to be light in the darkness. Will we dare to begin to believe and understand that the impact we can have is infinite because the God we serve is infinite?

We are called to be light to bring revelation, warmth, and enlightenment. Clarity comes with exposure to light. We can only see clearly when we are exposed to the light of the truth. As it is in the natural, so it is in the spiritual. We can bring revelation, truth, and clarity in the workplace only because we have received them from God.

Not only does light bring clarity and expel darkness, but it also brings warmth. If we choose to communicate the truth we have in a judgmental way, it will be cold, hard, and unlikely to be received. While it is absolutely true that only the conviction of the Holy Spirit and declaration of His Word truly touch the spirit of a man with spiritual truth, the way we communicate and the manner with which we communicate acts on the heart of man. Sometimes a harsh correcting word is required. But in the great majority of circumstances, genuine concern and heartfelt love communicate the heart of God with warmth.

Do not underestimate the power of just taking time to say hello, encourage, and take a genuine interest in the personal life of all your staff and colleagues, especially those others ignore. You will be amazed at the results. Let's endeavor to look for the opportunities and God-given appointments and be available to touch the hearts and lives of those around us. The Holy Spirit is with us, and He has a heart for the workplace and all the nonbelievers there. Do we make the most of our God-given opportunities every day? They are there literally every day.

"Because of the LORD's great love we are not consumed, for his compassions never fail. They are new every morning; great is your faithfulness" (LAM 3:22–23).

His mercies are new every morning. His plan was written for you on a daily basis and an hourly basis. There is no such thing as saints on ice. You cannot be benched in this game. If you are born again, you are in the game, or more correctly, you are in the war. This is a serious issue—one that has the eternal lives of people hanging in the balance.

It is not dependent on how you feel or the last time you consciously sinned, for if it were, we would all surely fail. It is based purely and simply on the affirmation we receive from God, Who says in Romans 8:1–2, *"Therefore, there is now no condemnation for those who are in Christ Jesus, because through Christ Jesus the law of the Spirit who gives life has set you free from the law of sin and death."*

We can walk into the very throne room of God with confidence, knowing that it is His righteousness and not ours that determines our position before our Creator. It is with this confidence and assurance that we need to operate to be effective in our witness.

Credibility

There is a credibility that comes from doing things God's way. Do it His way, and let Him determine the outcome. You cannot claim respect and honor. Credibility is not something you can engender unilaterally; other people attribute these desirable character traits to us. They are earned and cannot be demanded.

It is the difference between positional power and personal power. There are many people in authority who do not have respect. There are many people in a company who have respect and are not in positions of authority. If you want to understand credibility, then you need to understand this truth.

It is in what we do and how we act that these desirable attributes are born. It is the physical manifestation of the internal transformation that is the demonstration of the kingdom life. In other words, always, always, always walk the talk. If you do, you will engender respect and credibility.

It is only on this platform that you will have the trust and relationship required to speak truth powerfully into people's lives. It is a right that is earned, not imposed. As it is with most truth, the opposite also has an effect. If you don't walk the talk, you will reap disrespect and will lack credibility. Your words will then sound hollow. Workplace transformation always begins with personal transformation.

The most important business questions you can ask are: What are You doing, Lord? What do You want to do today? If we are not walking closely with God, if we are not hearing from Him, and if we are not discerning His will, then how can we be effective?

The example we have is our Lord and Savior. In John 14:12, He said we would do greater things than Him: *"I tell you the truth, anyone who has faith in me will do what I have been doing. He will do even greater things than these, because I am going to the Father."*

Mind-boggling though this is, it is a truth worth contemplating. We need to operate as He did, empowered by the Holy Spirit. He did none of these things in His own divinity. It was all in the power of the Holy Spirit.

How would our lives be transformed and our workplaces changed if we only did what we saw the Father doing? What radical places they would be. What an impact we would have. Oh that we would learn to walk as Jesus did, for in that is the power, love, and transformational potential that would radically impact our world. Will you dare to believe?

There is significant credibility to be gained by being a true team player. A successful business is the interaction of multiple tasks performed by many people. Valuing each member of a team regardless of his or her task or role ensures an inclusive culture and internal communication. As the Bible says in 1 Corinthians 12:14, *"For the body is not one member, but many"* (NASB).

Like any chain, an organization is only as strong as the weakest link. Often the hidden people doing seemingly mundane tasks are critical to a smooth, effective company. Public and private acknowledgment of their significance is not only the right thing to do—it also produces a wave of genuine productivity. The way we are seen to treat people and the honor and esteem we hold them in will directly translate into how effective our message and witness will be.

If there is one thing I have learned in business, it is this: always do it God's way and let Him decide the consequences. There is credibility that comes in doing things God's way. Do it His way, and let Him determine the outcome.

Our witness is determined in many ways. Ultimately it is God Who must do the convicting and bear witness to His own message. We can do nothing in our own strength, yet He has entrusted us with the message of salvation. We have the duty and wonderful privilege of being the messengers of good news to all mankind.

"How beautiful on the mountains are the feet of those who bring good news, who proclaim peace, who bring good tidings, who proclaim salvation, who say to Zion, 'Your God reigns!'" (Isa 52:7).

God has placed you deliberately wherever you are. It is no accident that you are in the workplace assigned to you. He has a plan and purpose, with daily tasks and opportunities specifically for you. You are the one who was chosen to expand the kingdom of God in your sphere of influence.

I encourage you to take the time to seek Him, acknowledge His presence in your workplace, and expect Him to move at your work.

Key Scripture

"But you shall receive power (ability, efficiency, and might) when the Holy Spirit has come upon you, and you shall be My witnesses in Jerusalem and all Judea and Samaria and to the ends (the very bounds) of the earth" (ACTS 1:8 AMP).

Main Points

- We are all called to witness.
- God is more interested in people than you are.
- We are called to demonstrate a transformed life.
- Is your Christian life attractive?
- Being salt and light is a choice.
- We all have influence at work.

Prayer

Make me Your witness to those You have placed around me, Lord. Give me a heart for the lost and an ear to hear what You are doing. Amen.

Notes

CHAPTER 6

WORK TO CREATE

"And if you call out for insight and cry aloud for understanding, and if you look for it as for silver and search for it as for hidden treasure, then you will understand the fear of the Lord and find the knowledge of God"

(PRO 2:3–5 NIV1984).

Our God is the creative God. He is the most creative thing in the whole universe. He even created creation. We are made in His image. Surely, we should be the most creative people in the world. We have the Creator of the universe in our hearts and access to the throne room of God, and we are empowered by the Holy Spirit. We are a potential fountain of creativity. If there is a problem to be overcome, a design to be engineered, or a solution to be found, then shouldn't the people of God have a reputation for providing the answers?

Our creativity is based not only on the gifting God has given us but also on our relationship with the great Creator. He is the Creator, but we are created in His image, to be like Him and to have His attributes and character. To see the fruit, though, we need to put our hand to the plow, but it is always He who creates the harvest.

So what is our responsibility in this area of creativity? How do we access this divine attribute? There is no doubt that we have been given a set of gifts and talents as unique as we are individual. Some people are more creative than others, but He has assigned us individually and appointed us specifically for a purpose. Within the parameters of our calling, there will be an aspect of creativity that can be applied.

Just as our gifts and talents need to be nurtured and developed, so it is with our creativity. We have a responsibility to enhance our natural propensity, but the source of our creativity can be inspired. It can be divine revelation as well as natural deduction. If we are to receive revelation, we need to have relationship. The relationship that leads to creativity, and the transformational revelation that ensues, is based on an unlikely partnership: you and God.

Are you equals? Of course not. Yet in His plan and purpose, He has chosen to work through His creation. Just as it is with witnessing, where we speak the words and the Holy Spirit convicts the person's heart, so it is with creativity. We need to put our hand to the plow if we want to be effective. We work hand in glove with the true source of all creativity.

There is a wonderful story told of two farmers in the middle of a drought. Both believed in God, and both prayed for rain. One man was out in his field crying out to God, tears rolling down his face in a genuine, heartfelt appeal to his Creator, standing in the dust of the drought-stricken field. The other man was doing exactly the same thing, with one definitive and life-changing difference: he was crying out while plowing his field.

Which one believed in his heart? Which one had faith? Which one received a harvest? When the rains came, only one had prepared. Note that God gave exactly the same thing to both men, and their circumstances were identical.

Do we have our hands to the plow at work? Are we plowing fields? Do we expect God to send the rain? These are big questions. Only you can answer them for yourself, but they are a constant challenge to me. It is only as we partner with God and do our part in faith, expecting Him to bring the creativity, the transformational power, and the overcoming answers, that we will see divine solutions to the issues we face and the opportunities we have.

Transformation

"We continually ask God to fill you with the knowledge of his will through all the wisdom and understanding that the Spirit gives" (COL 1:9).

Now we need to go a little deeper, beyond provision, witness, and personal transformation. What I am talking about in this chapter is co-creation with God as we partner in His purposes. This is all about teaming up with God.

I believe we can bring transformation to our sphere of influence. This is true regardless of your position, situation, or circumstances, whoever you are, wherever you are, and whatever you do. The

Lord's Prayer says in Matthew 6:10, *"Your kingdom come, your will be done, on earth as it is in heaven."*

What does the kingdom of God look like in your workplace? What can you do to help create it? While we go about our daily lives, we have an opportunity to never again see our daily grind as mundane, for if we partner with our Creator, we can see His transformational power and His kingdom come in our workplaces. If we will yield to Him in this way, He gives us His perspective as we work out His agenda.

I have seen Him turn around the worst of circumstances. He can move in a commercial environment that is almost beyond redemption, and restore profitability, growth, a positive culture, and success. I distinctly remember my first day in a new role looking at an almost impossible situation in a group of companies with major losses and so many problems it was almost overwhelming. Many were quick to say, "They will never change." It was a "bridge too far" and a "mission impossible,"

But with God all things are possible.

"I can do everything through him who gives me strength" (PHI 4:13 NIV1984).

Let's not super-spiritualize the Scriptures. They are practical, down-to-earth, and liberating on a day-to-day, real-world basis. As we apply the principles and mandates given to us by the Word of God, we will see fruit that goes beyond our understanding.

Each win we have, each sale we get, and every order that comes through the door has contributed to our success, and it has all been ordained and orchestrated by God. If we truly understood that truth, I wonder how thankful and prayerful we would be. God is truly with us every step of the way. When we get up in the morning, He is with us, and when we go to bed at night, He is with us. Take a little time to meditate on one of my favorite psalms. Let the truth of the Word wash your mind and renew your thinking.

"You have searched me, LORD, and you know me. You know when I sit and when I rise; you perceive my thoughts from afar. You discern my going out and my lying down; you are familiar with all my ways. Before a word is on my tongue you, LORD, know it completely. You hem me in behind and before, and you lay your hand upon me. Such knowledge is too wonderful for me, too lofty for me to attain. Where can I go from your Spirit? Where can I flee from your presence? If I go up to the heavens, you are there; if I make my bed in the depths, you are there. If I rise on the wings of the dawn, if I settle on the far side of the sea, even there your hand will guide me, your right hand will hold me fast. If I say, 'Surely the darkness will hide me and the light become night around me,' even the darkness will not be dark to you; the night will shine like the day, for darkness is as light to you" (Ps. 139:1–12).

We often believe that God is present and talk to Him accordingly in a specific quiet time or prayer time. But He doesn't go away in between these special times. His plan and His purpose are worked out all day, every day. Your nine-to-five job is the largest component of your day, and as such, it is arguably the most important to God. He is available in the seemingly mundane as well as the sacred and spectacular.

That sounds like a big call until you consider you will spend more time at work than doing anything else. Surely then as you are anointed and appointed for a purpose and God has a plan for your life, the core and basis of the outworking of that purpose will match the time allocated for it. Could it be that the works of service we are being prepared for are meant to be manifest at work?

You are ordained to have transformational power based on the relationship you have with God, and His creativity is placed in you to impact your workplace and help create the kingdom of God.

Imagine your workplace given an open heaven. What would God's plan for your colleagues be? Surely He has a heart to see them in relationship with Himself. He is also interested in the practical application of your everyday experience. He can bring transformation in many forms if we only take the time to ask Him in.

Growth

One sign of a transformed workplace is growth. Healthy things grow. God is into growth. When we see a healthy plant or animal, it grows and flourishes. God will cause things to grow. As it is in the natural, so it is in the spiritual.

Healthy, balanced growth doesn't occur without some intervention. There is always some pruning involved. Sometimes things go backward before they go forward. Pruning is healthy. Cutting away what is not of God often looks like a big problem, but out of it comes a healthy foundation, a healthy plant, and good, strong future growth. Pruning unlocks true potential that cannot be realized any other way.

"And have you completely forgotten this word of encouragement that addresses you as a father addresses his son? It says, 'My son, do not make light of the Lord's discipline, and do not lose heart when he rebukes you, because the Lord disciplines the one he loves, and he chastens everyone he accepts as his son.' Endure hardship as discipline; God is treating you as his children. For what children are not disciplined by their father? If you are not disciplined—and everyone undergoes discipline—then you are not legitimate, not true sons and daughters at all. Moreover, we have all had human fathers who disciplined us and we respected them for it. How much more should we submit to the Father of spirits and live! They disciplined us for a little while as they thought best; but God disciplines us for our good, in order that we may share in his holiness. No discipline seems pleasant at the time, but painful. Later on, however, it produces a harvest of righteousness and peace for those who have been trained by it" (HEB 12:5–11).

Creating growth in business is maximizing resources and capturing and enhancing opportunity. Growth is a natural outcome of creativity, in the true sense of the word. When God creates, growth ensues. So it is with us as we seek to serve Him and be obedient. As we do this, we will see His fruit of growth.

We can literally partner with God in our business development. If I have been placed in a company, then I have a sphere of influence. Regardless of whatever position I hold, there is an opportunity to invite God into the things over which I have been given authority. He is willing and available. He wants to invade your workplace, but He chooses to be a gentleman and will wait to be asked. Ask Him in, and stand back! Oh, and just for the record, His ways are very rarely our ways. Hold on to your preconceptions lightly.

There is a virtuous cycle that occurs as growth is experienced. Growth brings with it momentum. Momentum brings with it growth. I am a great believer in momentum. If you can encourage and create a culture that inspires and contains growth, you will achieve momentum. Small issues disappear if you can create momentum in your business. We can create a culture that expects growth and high performance by teaming it with the empowerment of the people with a clear vision. This will create momentum that will overcome.

In John Maxwell's book *The 21 Irrefutable Laws of Leadership*, he compares momentum to a train.[7] When a train is moving quickly, it can burst through a thick, reinforced wall of concrete. The same train at a standstill can be rendered powerless by a small block of wood in front of the wheels. It is exactly the same train or company, but it is ineffective without momentum. He goes on to say that a company has a great capacity and capability to deal with problems easily when it has momentum. However, it is paralyzed without momentum, and small problems seem insurmountable.

When you have momentum and growth, you will have quality problems in handling growth, capital, cash flow, and capacity

---

7 *The 21 Irrefutable Laws of Leadership*, John Maxwell, 2007, Thomas Nelson.

constraints. These are good problems to have and ones to which God also has the answers.

Vision

In Proverbs 29:18, the Bible says, *"Where there is no revelation, the people cast off restraint; but blessed is the one who heeds wisdom's instruction."* Another translation says it this way: *"Where there is no vision, the people perish"* (KJV). There is definitely something important about clarity of purpose. If a clear clarion call is articulated, it empowers people to align their decision-making in a specific direction.

Vision can be stated in many ways; even unconventional and odd ways can be effective. But they must be understood and acted on in a real and practical sense. I really like Dilbert's (aka Scott Adams) definition of a mission statement: "A long, awkward sentence that demonstrates management's inability to think clearly."

Here are some great parameters for how your vision should be presented. It should be written down; if it is in your head, no one can see it. Make it plain; keep it very simple so that it is memorable, and make it available to everyone. Those who pass by should be able to access it, so keep it available and in plain view. Keep it simple so it is easily understood; you don't need big words to be credible. Keep it short so it is understood quickly. Where did I get these guidelines? It comes from the Word of God.

"And the Lord answered me and said, write the vision and engrave it so plainly upon tablets that everyone who passes may be able to read it easily and quickly" (HAB 2:2 AMP).

How clear is your vision statement, company mission or purpose, or whatever you choose to call it? Test it against the mandate above. There is a lot of godly wisdom in a plain, simple, easily read, available, clear vision.

But what if you're not a leader of a business? A vision or mission doesn't necessarily have to be a part of a full company mandate. You can have a vision for what you do. It just needs to be inspired by God. Spending time with Him asking Him what He wants to do is the true basis of an empowered vision.

If you know what God wants to do, then you will have a lot of confidence to ask Him for what you need to achieve it. Taking the time to hear from Him is important in all aspects of your work. You may be surprised at what you hear. Most of the time we constrain ourselves to our own capabilities rather than opening up our potential by calling on God for help.

A clear vision is a statement of direction or more correctly perhaps an unattainable endpoint. However, it is a direction nonetheless. The power of having a clear direction contained within an empowered culture unlocks innovation and potential. It is very important to know where you're going.

"She gives no thought to the way of life; her paths wander aimlessly, but she does not know it" (Pro 5:6).

Where are you going, what are you trying to achieve, and what is the future state of your company you are aiming to get to? We all need direction in order to focus, allocate resources, and create vision and momentum. If we don't know where we are going, how will we know when we get there?

Don't be aimless and wander. Ask God for clarity of direction. Part of our destiny is orchestrated, and for part of it we need to partner with God, hear from Him, and impact our circumstances with faith, prayer, and action.

How can we be obedient if we do not hear, and how can we hear if we do not listen? That seems so obvious, but in the cold, hard reality of a brutal commercial environment, do we really take the time to hear from God?

Perhaps this is something that is just beginning to enter your consciousness as you read this book. You may well have walked with God for a long time, and you may have heard from Him before, but you can go deeper and walk a daily walk hearing from your Father.

Prayer

Prayer is vital to all aspects of creative transformation. To co-create we have to hear from God. We ought to expect this in business, just as we would expect a missionary or pastor to hear from God.

There are many ways we can hear from God and be guided by Him. We can be led by circumstance, a *rhema* word, the counsel of other people, the "still, small voice," a sense of inner peace, dreams, visions, and even visitations. It is written in Joel 2:28, *"And afterward, I will pour out my Spirit on all people. Your sons and daughters will prophesy, your old men will dream dreams, your young men will see visions."* Personally I would prefer to have dreams rather than visions although I am arguably chronologically predisposed to visions. God is still in the business of leading His people as He always has done.

If all this is a bit new for you or if you haven't heard from God for a while, why not ask God to give you a revelation of purpose? Ask Him, "Who am I? What do You want me to do? What is my place? What are You doing here, today, right now?"

There are positional and transformational, foundational prayers. These are spending time with God to understand who you are in Him and what He has planned and purposed for your life. While this is often a lifelong pursuit in its own right, He will reveal enough for your next steps, and it will be in line with your passions.

Other prayers are more mundane, if there is such a thing. There is a practical application of God's wisdom that stands us in good stead, and then there is the revelatory nature of His insight. What is revelation? It is just an insight from God. Where do those good ideas really come from?

Just think about the ramifications of that reality. Imagine having access to someone who knows everything, sees everything, knows everyone, and can see into the future. All the children of God should hear from their Father. This is not a gift for a chosen few; it is a path on which we all can and need to walk.

We absolutely have the privilege of being able to commune with God, yet we tend to take it for granted. If you need some direction in your business or workplace, He is vitality interested in your work life. Imagine the opportunity to talk with the ultimate business guru. Would you go out of your way for an hour with Buffet or Gates? Well, you have access to someone far, far superior, better connected, and infinitely more capable. Why not spend some time with Him and get your revelation?

Hearing from God

"But when he, the Spirit of truth, comes, he will guide you into all the truth. He will not speak on his own; he will speak only what he hears, and he will tell you what is yet to come" (JOHN 16:13).

In order to be effective in our business, we need to hear from God. If we are surrendered to Him and recognize His desire to be involved in the marketplace, then we should expect His guidance. He is interested in talking with us; it is not something we have to strive for.

Throughout the Bible, people walked and talked with God. They heard instructions, affirmations, discipline, and words from and for others. Often the instructions were very precise and contained a lot of detail. Some were moved through circumstances initiated by God while others saw angels, dreamed dreams, had visions, or simply received godly counsel.

If God is *"the same yesterday and today and forever,"* as the Bible says in Hebrews 13:8, then we should expect to hear from Him. Often He is guiding and leading, directing and initiating, and we are just wandering around blissfully unaware. However, He is calling us to intimacy, to walk with Him, to hear from Him, and to minister to those around us out of the resources He gives to us. So how does that work out in practice? May I offer some simple steps I have experienced and seen others use to begin to walk in this way?

First surrender your work life to God, invite Him in, and then expect Him to take an interest. We all operate from a worldview that will affect our observations and translations of what we see, hear, and experience. Our brains filter out information all the time. Our senses take in far more than we can focus on. Take, for example, when you buy a new car. You will instantly see all the other vehicles on the road that are similar to yours that previously you didn't even notice. It all depends on what you are focused on. The same goes for God's hand at work. You will see His influence in your workplace if you expect to see it and are focused on Him.

Let's consider some ways God can and will talk with us about business. If you have now surrendered or committed your business to God, He will arrange the circumstances.

"Paul and his companions traveled throughout the region of Phrygia and Galatia, having been kept by the Holy Spirit from preaching the word in the province of Asia" (ACTS 16:6).

Look for coincidences in your day—unexpected answers or contacts. Look for the seemingly prearranged. Notice also the doors that will not open. Some are to be pushed and others to be left alone. Look for the hand of God. Paul in this Scripture was hindered from going into Asia and took that as God shutting the door.

Listen to the quiet sense of inner peace and the still, small voice of the Holy Spirit communing with your Spirit. Do you feel really uncomfortable about a deal or opportunity? Learn to take note of your sense of peace from a positive and in a cautionary sense.

God will show you His will in more direct ways as well. You will be amazed at how directly He can guide you. It is no different from the first church and early apostles who were preaching the gospel in the marketplaces of the Middle East.

"I will instruct you and teach you in the way you should go; I will counsel you with my loving eye on you" (Psa 32:8).

It is almost mind boggling to try to understand why an infinite and almighty God would want to commune with His creation. He does so not as an odd event but on an ongoing basis with those who have been born again, which is accomplished the simple acknowledgment of sin, acceptance of Jesus as Savior, and surrender to Him as Lord.

There are ways other than hearing through circumstances and inner peace. Here are some more direct ways He can lead and guide you. A rhema word can be a Scripture that really impacts you. If you read your Bible regularly, ask the Holy Spirit to highlight His will for you. Often a verse will almost leap of the page or certainly draw your attention significantly. If you experience this, then ask the Holy Spirit to reveal what He wants to say to you through this word.

Sometimes someone will be speaking and you will be struck by a phrase of sentence that is highlighted to you. Again ask God if He is saying something to you. These revelation-type experiences and words are often a final confirmation of a decision or an important direction that you already have peace about and the circumstances have all lined up.

However, don't discount more dramatic interventions from God. He can and does speak through prophecy, dreams, visions, and even angels. It's not as crazy as it sounds. We are on an important mission and in a spiritual battle for souls. These are high on God's agenda, and He will intervene as He sees fit when we are submitted to His will and surrendered to His lordship.

I have learned to more highly value the input of others over the years. Don't underestimate godly counsel and listening to those God has placed around you. He has put them there for a reason.

Some who have been there before can bring a word of wisdom or insight.

If we become like Him, we can be effective ambassadors for Him. Our message is not physical but spiritual. It is spiritually discerned, and we need to be led, empowered, and indwelt by the Spirit to be effective. The goal is to have the mind of Christ. That is not us becoming zombies; far from it. It is the fulfillment of all our potential and becoming all He intended us to be.

"The Spirit searches all things, even the deep things of God. For who knows a person's thoughts except their own spirit within them? In the same way no one knows the thoughts of God except the Spirit of God. What we have received is not the spirit of the world, but the Spirit who is from God, so that we may understand what God has freely given us. This is what we speak, not in words taught us by human wisdom but in words taught by the Spirit, explaining spiritual realities with Spirit-taught words. The person without the Spirit does not accept the things that come from the Spirit of God but considers them foolishness, and cannot understand them because they are discerned only through the Spirit. The person with the Spirit makes judgments about all things, but such a person is not subject to merely human judgments, for, 'Who has known the mind of the Lord so as to instruct him?' But we have the mind of Christ" (1 COR 2:10–16).

If only my thoughts were aligned to God's will. How good would that be? If only I had the insight and awareness of His perfect will. Take a look at this Scripture in Proverbs 16:3: *"Roll your works upon the Lord [commit and trust them wholly to Him; He will cause your thoughts to become agreeable to His will, and] so shall your plans be established and succeed"* (AMP).

Can that really be true? Could it really be that simple? If we cast our works onto Him and commit and trust them to Him, He will make us think along the lines of His will. Why? So your plans will work, and you will have success!

That is staggering in its significance. If we trust Him, He will turn our hearts to His will. We know that if we are in His will, He will guide us and lead us. How comforting it is to know that as we commit our works to Him, He will turn us to not only hear from Him, but our very thoughts will become His thoughts. Then we will truly have the mind of Christ.

"Commit your works to the Lord and your plans will be established" (PRO 16:3 NASB).

When you are making plans, the same principle applies. Invite God into what you are doing. He may well have a different agenda. Prayerfully consider any important decision, and seek the wise counsel of others.

Make a point of committing your works to God. Offer them up to Him in a specific, definite way you are comfortable with. Doing this will allow His blessing to fall and His wisdom to prevail. It will also give you confidence that He is in control. You will see opportunities you didn't see before and be amazed at the way things begin to line up. When times are tough, you will know God is with you as you have committed your business to Him.

Why not take the time to pray right now? "Father, I commit my workplace to You. Lead me, guide me, and establish my plans according to Your will and word; in the name of Jesus, amen."

Intercessional praying is praying on purpose, for a purpose. We have very much focused on His will for us; here is an opportunity to bring others and their circumstances to Him. In a marketplace context, that is as valid as it is in church.

Jesus preached, reached, and had compassion for those outside the church. He operated in the marketplace, roads, businesses, streets, and homes of unbelievers. Everything we have talked about in regard to our own circumstances and hearing from God also applies to others. We are called to be a blessing, and we can use the authority we have been given to create life in another's circumstances as we ask for heavenly blessing and intervention into the lives of those around us. God loves them enough to die for them, just as He did for us. He left His sternest remarks for the religious people of the day, something we should continually bear in mind as we bear His name.

Reconciliation

Here is an aspect of creation that you may not see as creative. We can create reconciliation. It is aligned with our role as salt and light. It is creative in because it forms new relationships, but the execution of the solution is also an opportunity to demonstrate God's insight and creativity. This is not something for the specialists. You don't have to where a hair shirt and eat locusts and honey to be used in this way. We are all called to the ministry of reconciliation, for blessed are the peacemakers. There are plenty of opportunities for exercising this in any business!

"All this is from God, who reconciled us to himself through Christ and gave us the ministry of reconciliation. That God was reconciling the world to himself in Christ, not counting people's sins against them. And he has committed to us the message of reconciliation" (2 COR 5:18–19).

What is it to have a ministry in reconciliation? In its pure form, it is leading others to Christ and them being reconciled to Him. But I believe the mandate is broader than that.

When we preach in church, we minister to a very small minority. When we demonstrate and communicate our faith in the marketplace, we are impacting a majority. If we are going to see a significant move of God with multitudes saved, it will be because we have taken the gospel out of the church and into the real world.

We have a mandate from Jesus and the example of His disciples who took the gospel out into the world. Let's aspire to live our lives showing the imprint of the God we serve. It is important that we demonstrate a transformed life. This is not for our own sake or in our own strength but yielded to a transforming God who will ensure we become more like Him.

"He who began a good work in you will carry it on to completion until the day of Christ Jesus" (Phi 1:6).

This dynamic is as applicable in large issues as it is in small ones. The power of influence today sits less with governments and more with business. Global business transcends borders, and the influence, both good and bad, of economics and trade dictates global stability and prosperity. Redeeming business should be a priority. The ministry of reconciliation can be from the smallest example of conflict between workmates in a micro company to large-scale creative economic reconciliation.

The recent global financial crisis is as much a crisis of faith as economics. We would be in a better state had the mantras of free trade and financial liberation been firmly contained in a framework of ethics, moderation, social conscience, and fiscal responsibility. Wouldn't that be a great world?

Your ministry can bring reconciliation to your family, business, staff and management, industry, and marketplace. Demonstrate ethics and generosity, go the extra mile, take the time to share your faith, and impact your environment for good. The Holy Spirit will empower you and guide you as you serve Him and His purpose in your call to business. You can literally create a positive environment and bring the kingdom of God to earth. That is the creative impact available to each of us.

In your daily experience of work, the ministry of reconciliation sounds like a grandiose title. But we often need to reconcile with ourselves and with those immediately around us. How do we handle those who would be at odds with us? Yes that includes your colleague who really annoys you and the overbearing boss. Unfortunately, God is always right, much though we would like to argue the point from time to time. His Word is clear when it says in 1 Peter 3:9, *"Do not repay evil with evil or insult with insult. On the contrary, repay evil with blessing, because to this you were called so that you may inherit a blessing."*

Bless those who curse me? Are you kidding? Seek out those who hate me and bless them? Are you insane? Repaying evil with good doesn't seem to make any sense, but God's ways are not our ways. He has a better view. If we have given our lives to Him, we need to trust Him and do it His way. It is not easy, and yes, it is a narrow path, but it is a higher way—a true and pure way.

Being motivated by a higher purpose should empower us to put aside our own petty issues and prejudices and work for the greater good. If we choose to do it God's way, we will get God's results, and they will always be better than ours.

Often reconciliation takes place between parties that would normally and naturally have animosity. How do we deal with those with whom we would not normally take the time to consider? Who will speak for those who do not or cannot speak for themselves? Who will right the injustices and reconcile the inequalities that pervade our workplace, marketplace, and society and yet go unchallenged?

"Speak up for those who cannot speak for themselves, for the rights of all who are destitute" (PRO 31:8).

If you are in a leadership position in business, God has given you influence. What will you use it for? Will you use it to bless yourself and your family? Yes, that is fine. Maybe you will use it to bless others in your company or church. That's fine too. But what of those who have no voice in society, those who have no influence or resources? Who will speak for them? How will their voices be heard, and how will justice be done?

You have received the Spirit of God regardless of your earthly position, so you have godly influence, wherever He has placed you. He has given you authority. Whether you are sweeping floors or a CEO, you are equal in God's eyes. You literally carry the anointing and presence of God. How much authority do you need?

"I have given you authority to trample on snakes and scorpions and to overcome all the power of the enemy; nothing will harm you" (LUK 10:19).

Often we see life through our own worldview, from our own perspective, blissfully unaware of others who are less fortunate than ourselves. It is our duty to look again and ask how we can help. You can make a difference. Exercise that ministry of reconciliation, and operate in the full creativity given to you by a creative God.

Favor

A good prayer life will bring us into favor—not only favor with God but also favor with man. These two things are not mutually exclusive. God will give us insights and opportunities with divine appointments. He is able to do all things. If only we knew the great favor we have with God, as we are seated at the His right hand.

We are in Christ. That astounding truth is beyond our imagination. We have a standing with God that is equal to Christ, for we are in Christ. We are washed clean by the blood of Jesus. When God looks at us, He doesn't see our failings; He sees the righteousness of Jesus Christ. This is not from anything we have done, but is purely, solely, and absolutely the outrageous grace and infinite mercy of our loving heavenly Father.

There is something about walking closely with God that creates an atmosphere. This can shift mindsets and circumstances. Sometimes just our presence in a place or situation can move opposition or bring resolution. This is no source of pride because it is not us; it is the Holy Spirit who indwells us, and His anointing can literally move mountains.

"The Lord was with him; he showed him kindness and granted him favor in the eyes of the prison warden" (GEN 39:21).

The Lord showed him kindness and favor. Which of us would not want more of that? We who are called to His purposes and surrendered to His will are able to solicit His favor. That can be manifested in many ways. Resistance can fall away, the hearts of those who oppose us can shift, and we can expect favor from those in authority over us. Be bold. Why not seek His will and ask for His favor? You may be surprised by just how willing He is to move on your behalf to accomplish His will.

With favor will come opportunities. Look for opportunities to be faithful. This is part of our personal growth, development, and transformational journey. God will place us in circumstances where we can demonstrate our growth and faithfulness, often in the mundane, unseen tasks. It is here that responsibility and faithfulness, which are precious in His sight, are developed. When we prove our faithfulness in small things, we are given greater opportunity.

"Well done, good and faithful servant! You have been faithful with a few things; I will put you in charge of many things. Come and share your master's happiness!" (MAT 25:21).

Would you like to share in the happiness of God? He is the Creator of all happiness, pleasure, and joy. Shared happiness is sign of intimacy and of a close relationship. What a beautiful picture of our Father's love for us. It is out of an understanding of that love and the overwhelming gift of His sacrifice that our faith and works are grounded in the workplace. It is not out of appeasing an angry, capricious being but in serving faithfully a loving and giving God.

When we have been proven faithful with a little, we will be given much more. It is a spiritual principle that I have seen outworked so clearly in the marketplace. We have God's unmerited favor. He has decided in His mercy and His grace to give us His favor. We have favor with Him not because of what we have done or who we are but because of His love, the sacrifice of His Son, and the position we hold, seated at the right hand of the Father in Christ.

Just as we have received the unmerited favor of God, He can cause us to receive favor from those in authority over us or any other stakeholders in our workplace. He has the ability to shift a man's heart and grant us favor. Such is the favor of God that He can open doors that no man can close, shift the heart that no man can open, and change the mind of the most obstinate person in the twinkling of an eye.

What a privilege it is to serve a God who wants the best for us. He is an omnipotent, omnipresent God to whom belongs honor and worship, yet He is a friend of the lowly and interested in the most humble person in the most intimate way.

"In the Lord's hand the king's heart is a stream of water that He channels toward all who please Him" (PRO 21:1).

God has the power to change a man's heart. He has the influence to give you favor among men and a willingness to open doors for His children. As His follower, you have a right to ask for His influence and favor. He may say no, or He may open a door that seems stuck fast. Often we do not know all God has for us, so we need to trust Him with the answers He gives.

Why not ask Him today and see Him empower you and your business as you seek to serve Him? The right favor at the right time can bring breakthrough change. Sometimes we look at an option and say, "That would never happen." But God is the God of the breakthrough, quite capable of moving a man's heart and giving you outrageous favor. Ask Him; you may be surprised at the outcome.

Insight

How often have we said, "If only I knew more about the situation. If only I knew what the other company was thinking, what the customers really needed, and what would make the stakeholders on the other side of the table come to the party"? What we often need is more insight. How good would it be to know everything, to understand everything, to read motivation and behavior, to see the future, to understand the past, to know the real motivation of a man's heart, and to see the intricacies of the situation with a global view? There is only One Who has that view, yet we have access to Him.

We will never be able to see as much as God sees, and He will never give us a completely transparent view. His ways are not our ways, and He has purposes and plans that we only see dimly. However, if we have an intimate relationship with God, we are able to discern things we would not normally be able to see. On occasion, as He wills, we will be given insight beyond normal comprehension as He exercises favor to perfect His will in our lives and the lives of those around us.

What an unspeakable privilege it is to be able to hear from our heavenly Father, Who is so loving and intimate yet so overwhelmingly mighty. We do serve an awesome God.

"And if you call out for insight and cry aloud for understanding, and if you look for it as for silver and search for it as for hidden treasure, then you will understand the fear of the Lord and find the knowledge of God" (PRO 2:3 NIV1984).

There is an essence in this Scripture that understanding and wisdom need to be toiled for, as one would search for gold or silver. There is a measure of discipline, sweat, dedication, and work required. Will we pay the price for insight beyond our realm of understanding? Will we seek the wisdom of God? What a privilege it is to have access to the throne room of unfathomable grace.

In David McCracken's book *An Incorruptible Heart*, he wonderfully demonstrates the difference between Saul and David. He explains that whereas Saul was anointed because of his role, David was anointed because of his heart. What a staggering insight. The intimacy of David's relationship with God made him eligible to receive a king's anointing, whereas Saul's anointing was given so he could exercise a role. There is a world of difference between the two.

McCracken goes on to exhort us to build intimacy with God through *"transparency with the Father, hunger for His presence, and obedience to His daily directives, diligence in prayer and consistency in the study and application of His word."*[8]

These are basic things that are so easily forgotten in our busy lives and daily routines, yet as David McCracken has so powerfully put it, these things build intimacy and our relationship with God. They give us not only the anointing but also insight based in relationship and favor. If we are truly to hear from God in our daily walk, it will be built on the daily disciplines of learning to be intimate and taking the time to incline our ear and hear from Him.

Restoration

There is something powerful in the concept of restoration—the restoring of all things that are good. Where there has been loss, there will be gain, where there has been sickness there will be wellness, and where there has been shortfall, there will be abundance.

The restoration of what has been stolen or lost—the very concept is intrinsically right. Restoration is a fundamental principle underlining the very foundation of God's kingdom. In the Lord's Prayer we are exhorted to pray, "Your kingdom come, Your will be done on earth as it is in heaven." It is the restoration of life on earth to become like life in heaven.

Our God is the God of restoration. Since the beginning of time, the plan was hatched to restore humankind to Himself through the death of His Son. This is the ultimate example and demonstration of restoration. It is pure restoration, born of love from the Father's heart and out of His very nature and character.

---

8   *An Incorruptible Heart,* David McCracken, 2010, David McCracken Ministries.

The Bible is full of stories of restoration. It is one of the great characteristics of God. If we are to see His kingdom built in our workplaces, then we will see restoration. Restoration in people, relationships, finances, culture, and all aspects of work life are evidence of His hand at work.

We are sinful people, and we work in sinful environments. Our workplaces and the broader marketplace, by their very natures, manifest a fallen state. Our task as Christians in being salt and light is to restore what has fallen, including relationships, standards, people, and all we encounter in the power of God for the restoration of His kingdom.

God is in the restoration business. He can and does restore hearts, lives, families, and fortunes. He can restore your business when all seems lost. Lives get changed when He is around. Sometimes He can restore "before your very eyes."

"'I will give you honor and praise among all the peoples of the earth when I restore your fortunes before your very eyes,' says the Lord" (ZEP 3:20).

He can bring healings, miracles, radical restoration, godly reconstruction, and instant reconciliation. Nothing and no one is beyond God's ability to restore—no person, no business, and no situation. It sounds simple, but sometimes we just forget how big He really is.

In other circumstances, it can be a long, demanding, slow, and boring process. In these circumstances, discernment is a vital weapon in our armory. We need to hear from God and discern whether we are to fight or to endure. Fighting a battle not meant to be fought will just tire you out.

In our own strength we can do nothing, and yet Philippians 4:13 says, *"I can do everything through him who gives me strength"* (NIV1984). It is in our weakness that He will prevail. When we don't rely on ourselves but rely totally on Him, then His true strength is manifest in us.

"But he said to me, 'My grace is sufficient for you, for my power is made perfect in weakness.' Therefore I will boast all the more gladly about my weaknesses, so that Christ's power may rest on me" (2 Cor 12:9).

Sometimes the challenges do seem overwhelming, but nothing is impossible to God. He is the God of the breakthrough; He is the one who will restore all things to Himself.

"'At that time I will gather you; at that time I will bring you home. I will give you honor and praise among all the peoples of the earth when I restore your fortunes before your very eyes,' says the Lord" (Zep 3:20).

It is a privilege to minister restoration into the workplace and to be the vehicle of God. We can be a part of His plan to see His kingdom expanded. When this happens, the workplace becomes more equitable and more reasonable—a place where people want to be that is effective and efficient. We all have a calling to bear fruit in our area of influence.

As we move with creative intent and listen to the promptings of the Holy Spirit, we unlock heavenly influence and insight, and we will indeed see the establishment of His influence and kingdom. There will be ideas and innovations, breakthroughs and growth. We will see reconciliation and restoration as we move in humble obedience to the Father's promptings. What a privilege it is to serve a God who is willing to partner with us mere mortals to serve His purposes.

Key Scripture

> *"And if you call out for insight and cry aloud for understanding, and if you look for it as for silver and search for it as for hidden treasure, then you will understand the fear of the Lord and find the knowledge of God" (Pro 2:3–5).*

Main Points

- We have the creative power of God.
- We are empowered to transform.
- We have the mind of Christ.
- Good things grow.
- We need to hear to be obedient.
- We are ministers of reconciliation.
- God is in the restoration business.

Prayer

Lord, help me to hear from You and act on what You say. Bring Your transformation to my workplace, and may Your kingdom come.

Notes

CHAPTER 7

WORK TO WORSHIP

"Whatever you do, work at it with all your heart, as working for the Lord, not for human masters"

(COL 3:23).

When I use the word worship, what do you think of? What image comes to mind? Does it conjure up pictures of a beautiful building and choirs? Maybe you think of crowds of people raising their hands and singing to God, or perhaps a scene of quiet, prayerful reflection and adoration. Our usual response is to see this in a church setting and to equate worship with a sanctified setting, and there is nothing wrong with that. However, worship in its true sense goes far beyond collective singing on a Sunday.

Worship is also a victim of the perception of a secular-sacred divide. We have, as with so much of our expression of Christianity, locked worship into the Sunday service. True worship of God is not only a time of singing with others in church but also how we live our lives, the attitude and position of our hearts, and the surrender and obedience of the human spirit submitted to the lordship of Jesus Christ. Worship and business are not usually closely associated.

Avodah

What if I told you that work and worship in the Bible were so closely aligned that a single word would describe both? How far have we come from that? It is a concept that is almost completely foreign to our modern Western Christian walk. Yet it is a biblical truth that needs to be restored to the people of God.

Avodah is a Hebrew word that occurs regularly in Scripture. It is at the foundation of all it is to serve and praise our God. The word is mostly translated as *worship* yet its other meaning is *work*. It's the same word with two meanings.

Could our mundane work life really be an act of worship? We worship as we surrender to His will. This literally brings His lordship into the workplace, the very kingdom of God, and where the kingdom of God is, there is worship.

As we walk openhearted before Him, giving Him glory, hearing His voice, and endeavoring to do all things with excellence, with a heart that is open and surrendered before Him, we do indeed worship.

"Whatever you do, work at it with all your heart, as working for the Lord, not for human masters" (COL 3:23).

We have intellectualized so much about Christianity that we may be concerned about having a heart response, but the experience of the presence of God is a vital part of our walk with Him. So much of that experience is locked away as we have become educated and chosen a postmodern, intellectualized path peppered with good Greek philosophy that has downgraded and denied our feelings.

We can tune our hearts, to sense the presence of God, not only during a time of corporate worship, but every day as we walk and work and worship. Can work and worship be the same thing? Your workplace is your place of worship. As you serve God in excellence and learn to see Him in all you do, you worship. God is in all things.

Surrender

Surrendering our will to God is an integral part of what it means to serve and follow Jesus. In making Him Lord, we are willing to do His bidding and follow His plan. This unleashes the power of God in our lives because He will only operate in the heart of a surrendered person. This is defined by His desire to give us free will so we will not be robots but will choose to love and serve Him freely.

Surrender does not mean turning off of our brains. We are given an intellect and wisdom to choose well and rightly in the circumstances in which we find ourselves. But the position of our will in surrender to Him has an essence of worship. It is a yielding of ourselves as sacrifices as we place our lives on the altar and surrender to His purposes.

There is, however, a deeper way that involves our heart, not just our will. This is more than intellectual assent to a surrendered life; it is the positioning of our hearts toward receiving from Him. It is a place of adoration.

I have been learning to "practice the presence of God." This is where I tune my heart to be deliberately aware of God's presence. As I yield in this way, I can sense His presence just as I have done in church during a time of worship or personal prayer.

As you do this, you can literally change an atmosphere. You are opening your immediate environment to the palpable presence of God. I have seen many meetings shift as I open myself up to the Spirit in a meeting. This is not freaky. It should be quite normal to just be aware of His presence and yield to Him. It brings His favor and purposes to bear. It is powerful—very powerful.

Brother Lawrence was a lowly monk in the 17th century who wrote about and "practiced the presence of God." He found worship in serving others and in the simplest of tasks. His letters are now part of the pivotal writings of church history and of how to walk with God at work.

His real name was Nicholas Herman, which sounds a little less religious and says more about who he really was. But Nick found he could sense God's presence in the mundane and the menial; now that is true worship. True humility is love, and true love is hearing and being obedient to God, for God is love.

Surrendering to God in this way allows your heart to become sensitive to hearing His voice. Like any discipline, it takes time and practice to remember to be aware. His promptings are not always obvious, and we need to learn to discern His will. This positioning of our heart seems almost insignificant, yet in my experience it is the single most important way of discerning God's will and experiencing His impact in our lives.

However, this has to be complemented by being steeped in the Word. The Word will always confirm the Spirit. We would also be wise to walk closely with those around us, that we not be tempted and go astray. Surrounding ourselves with people who also walk with God is a great leveler and balance.

Humility

I think the concept of humility is probably one of the most misunderstood in our Christian walk. We tend to think that in some way it requires the downgrading of self. A Christian life is not one where we need to be a doormat, be taken advantage of, or slavishly deny ourselves and operate with a low self-esteem.

Humility—true humility—is valuing others and valuing ourselves in an understanding of God's love and His heart for us all. If we have a healthy self-esteem based on an understanding of the value God places on us, we are in a place to serve those who are around us. True humility is walking with God, having surrendered our lives to His purposes.

False humility is often a show, where people are proud of their humility. That sounds like a contradiction, but it's not. It is often associated with religion. Religion is not the true practice the following Jesus but a false set of rules, practices, and customs that have a form of godliness but deny its power.

True Christianity is surrendering your life to Jesus Christ and following Him as your Lord. Religion is where men aspire and reach for God; true Christianity is where God reaches down for us and lifts us up to be all we can be.

It is the reassurance, and the assurance, of knowing a loving Savior that gives us the sense of purpose, grace, and power to be humble and to accept what God says about us. Yes, we need a Savior, and yes, we are sinful. But He has paid the price for that sin. We are forgiven and seated at the right hand of God in Christ Jesus. The full measure of our humility is the alignment of our lives and our hearts to the purposes of God. More than that, it is an agreement with what He says about us despite how we may perceive ourselves.

Often humility can look anything but humble. Sometimes it is about not shrinking back, and sometimes it can look like pride. Take David, for instance, who was a young boy tending sheep left behind to do the menial domestic chores while his older brothers went to war. The war was not going well, with the opposition having Goliath in its ranks. When David came to bring lunch to his brothers, he saw and heard a giant Philistine cursing God.

Something stirred up in David—an angry, righteous indignation that said this should not be—and he challenged Goliath to the one-sided battle. What would that have looked like to his brothers? What must that have looked like to the army of God who assembled every morning and didn't engage the enemy? Who did he think he was? He was just a boy, yet he thought he could take on an enemy that the bravest warrior in Israel would not. We all know the wonderful story of when David went out to meet his enemy; he had this cry on his lips.

"You come against me with sword and spear and javelin, but I come against you in the name of the Lord Almighty, the God of the armies of Israel, whom you have defied. This day the Lord will deliver you into my hands, and I'll strike you down and cut off your head. This very day I will give the carcasses of the Philistine army to the birds and the wild animals, and the whole world will know that there is a God in Israel. All those gathered here will know that it is not by sword or spear that the Lord saves; for the battle is the Lord's, and He will give all of you into our hands" (1 Sam 17:45–47).

David was a man who was humble. He was a man submitted to God, who knew the battle is the Lord's. He gave glory to God and moved in His strength, courage, and anointing. His willingness to be obedient and the positioning of his heart in surrender to God's will, coupled with the empowering of the Holy Spirit, led to a great victory.

David moved in true humility, against the prevailing opinion of those around him. In fact, even those who knew him well, including his brothers, mistook his humility for pride. They thought he was conceited, prideful, and filled with false motivation. This was a reflection of their own hearts, and not a true description of David's.

"*When Eliab, David's oldest brother, heard him speaking with the men, he burned with anger at him and asked, 'Why have you come down here? And with whom did you leave those few sheep in the wilderness? I know how conceited you are and how wicked your heart is; you came down only to watch the battle'*" (1 SAM 17:28).

When you walk in true humility, you're walking in worship. When you work in true humility, you are working in worship. Don't expect those around you, even those who are very close to you, to understand or interpret your actions correctly. Let your confidence be in God, and always do it His way and let Him decide the consequences.

Obedience

To hear and obey is worship. In John 14:15, Jesus says that love and obedience are inseparable: "*If you love me, you will obey what I command.*" We often equate love with soft, sentimental feelings, yet true love is as much an action as a feeling. It is love that motivates us into being obedient and subservient to the One Who loved us first. It is out of an intimacy with Him that we begin to understand His heart toward us and our hearts react to Him.

"*What good is it, my brothers and sisters, if someone claims to have faith but has no deeds? Can such faith save them? Suppose a brother or a sister is without clothes and daily food. If one of you says to them, 'Go in peace; keep warm and well fed,' but does nothing about their physical needs, what good is it? In the same way, faith by itself, if it is not accompanied by action, is dead*" (JAM 2:14–17).

But just as faith without works is dead, so too blind obedience without a heart motivated by compassion can be heavy-handed and unsympathetic. Obedience is synonymous with worship because a heart of worship motivates obedience. Our obedience is evidence of an internal motivation that is grounded in love and surrendered to Him.

The promptings we receive from the Spirit, when acted on, can have a profound effect not only on us but also on those around us. The life of our businesses and workplaces can be significantly impacted by our worship in the form of obedience. This goes beyond a general understanding of what it is to lead a Christian life. It is not the implementation of good morals or following a bunch of rules but a day-by-day walk with God where we rely not only on the general principles in His Word but also on the daily promptings of the Spirit with Whom we walk.

I would encourage you to walk in this way. It is an adventure but one that is rewarding beyond all measure. The assurance of a loving Savior becomes palpable as you trust in Him each day, aware that He is intimately interested in all you do. What a privilege to be able to walk hand in hand with the Master. This model is not new; it was demonstrated by Jesus. He walked not in His own divinity but at His father's bidding, under the guidance, anointing, and prompting of the Holy Spirit.

"Jesus gave them this answer: 'I tell you the truth, the Son can do nothing by himself; he can do only what he sees his Father doing, because whatever the Father does the Son also does'" (JOHN 5:19 NIV1984).

It is this walk that needs to be emulated if we are to walk like Jesus did. He challenged us with a mind-blowing concept that we could do greater things than He did.

"I tell you the truth, anyone who has faith in me will do what I have been doing. He will do even greater things than these, because I am going to the Father" (JOHN 14:12).

This kind of obedience can seem to be quite threatening. If you're anything like me, you may become concerned that these might be your own thoughts, distractions, and desires. Then every so often you act on impulse when you believe God has spoken, and find that God He really has. I have experienced specific insights into people's lives that when I acted on them, moved them significantly.

Other examples are a lot more mundane, and often we ignore the signs or just write them off. Have you had someone on your mind recently? We all experience this, and just maybe God is saying something.

If you are experiencing this, then why not ask God why is this person is on your mind? You may need to pray and hold him or her up before God. Perhaps the person needs a word of encouragement; you could wait on God for a Scripture to give to him or her. These are simple things we can do to align ourselves to the will of God and to be actively involved in seeing His kingdom established.

When we have considered God at work, we may think that He is only interested in personal salvation and not the seemingly mundane mechanics of our work life. In my experience, it is often both.

Once I was sitting at my computer writing a report. Since I am a hands-on, active, big-picture person, this is not one of my favorite endeavors. In the midst of my concentration, a stray thought entered my mind. We had been dealing with an issue in Japan where a major supplier was experiencing significant business problems. These circumstances had led to the freezing of over a million dollars that was owed to us. We had tried all the usual channels and had no success in getting the funds released.

The general manager in charge of that business unit was an occasional churchgoer. We had never really talked together about Christian things, but we had a good working relationship. He was very concerned, as we all were, about what looked like a significant loss.

The thought that came into my mind was to go and pray with the gentleman in question about the issue in Japan. My 'Spirit-filled, man of God' response was, "You have to be joking, don't you?" All the usual, natural responses kicked in: What would he think? Was it appropriate? Was it just me? What if nothing happened?

The nice thing about serving a gracious God is that at the right time, He gives you just enough courage to make the right decision.

I went and knocked on the door of the manager. I stumbled about in general conversation before suggesting that since he went to church on albeit rare occasions, had he thought about praying for the situation in Japan? His surprised response was, "No, why?" I suggested that perhaps we could pray together and see what happened. He agreed, and we prayed.

I went back to my desk greatly concerned that God would let me down. I was more worried about my own reputation than His. They say that the size of faith needed to move mountains is just a mustard seed, yet my faith in the situation was so much smaller. Yet I had to trust God, be obedient to the prompting, and wait out the result, leaving the consequences to Him.

The next morning, I heard this strident voice coming down the corridor, saying, "It worked, it worked!" God had moved on our behalf in another nation, and the funds were released in full. He had addressed a major need, overcome an impossible situation, and strengthened the faith of two men who dared to ask Him to intervene in their work.

I've seen this happen so many times in the small, seemingly insignificant promptings that often have an impact. Sometimes it is significant, and other times it is over something small. But in God's economy, sometimes the small things are the most important. In this area, the Word says in Luke 16:10 that He who is trustworthy in the small things will be trusted with bigger things: *"Whoever can be trusted with very little can also be trusted with much."*

Excellence

We are called to demonstrate a higher standard. We are instructed to do all things in excellence, as serving the Lord.

"Hezekiah carried out this work and kept it up everywhere in Judah. He was the very best—good, right, and true before his God. Everything he took up, whether it had to do with worship in God's Temple or the carrying out of God's Law and Commandments, he did well in a spirit of prayerful worship. He was a great success" (2 CHR 31:20–21 MSG).

Walking in excellence is honoring and worshipping God. We are called not only to a high standard but the highest standard in all we do. Why? Because we serve the King of Kings. He has called us to a higher way and to be all we can be. If we are saved, we know the forgiveness of God. It is in this heartfelt appreciation that we should serve, walking as Hezekiah did in a "spirit of prayerful worship." This resulted in excellence.

It is not in the dogmatic slavery of submission to a capricious deity that we exist; it is in the loving, heartfelt pursuit of He who first loved us and gave His life, that we might know Him.

The excellence we strive for should be the natural fruit of a thankful heart, not a sense of duty. I think that collectively we have largely failed to recognize God's plan and purpose for our work, and in doing so, we have lost the worshipful joy and purpose of serving Him in the marketplace. If we regain that sense of purpose, we regain again the joy of service and the desire for excellence.

We are called to excellence in all areas of our lives. In as much as it applies to our work life, it should be obvious in all areas of our daily existence. As Christians, we should be renowned in our area of expertise and service. We should be the "go-to guys," the ones to be trusted and who always do a good job. Our lives should be a clear demonstration of changed lives that have been impacted by the Creator of all that is good.

We should demonstrate excellence in planning, excellence in relationships, and excellence in application. With all due respect to my adopted home in Australia, there is no room for the local colloquialism, "She'll be right, mate," in the kingdom of God.

If we are indeed, as I have said many times in this book, "anointed and appointed for a purpose," then our gifting and His empowerment should stand out as we submit our lives to Him to fulfill His purposes.

The Bible says in Colossians 3:23, *"Whatever you do, work at it with all your heart, as working for the Lord, not for human masters."* Therein lies the key to success. Study and meditate on that one verse, and it will transform your life. It is the cornerstone of attitude, surrender, integrity, and industry. Imagine what would happen if we really applied that to our work life. Would we be more productive, effective, industrious, honest, efficient, conscientious, and successful? I think we would; I know we would.

I really do enjoy excellence. I appreciate seeing things done well, professionally, efficiently, and effectively. A well-conceived idea that is powerfully executed and delivered is great to experience. I have had the privilege of working with teams who have strived for excellence and brought significant change in organizations that were struggling. It is great to be a part of something that is successful, well managed, engaging, and changing for good.

God calls us to strive for excellence by working with all our hearts, being passionate and committed. Sometimes that is not easy. We will not be successful in all we do. This is an important thing to remember. We will fall, we will fail, and our attitude under these circumstances and our response to them should still demonstrate a servant heart, God-honoring behavior, and the pursuit of excellence. Difficult times can be caused by our own actions or by those around us. Sometimes God will allow circumstances to prevail against us for a season, but He has always has a reason. You will ultimately overcome and be strengthened.

"Do you not know? Have you not heard? The LORD is the everlasting God, the Creator of the ends of the earth. He will not grow tired or weary, and his understanding no one can fathom. He gives strength to the weary and increases the power of the weak. Even youths grow tired and weary, and young men stumble and fall; but those who hope in the LORD will renew their strength. They will soar on wings like eagles; they will run and not grow weary, they will walk and not be faint" (Isa 40:28–31).

Trouble comes in many forms. In particular we are not to look necessarily to our earthly masters. They may be a board, a company owner, a CEO, or whatever. You may disagree; they may be incompetent, inexperienced, rude, or overbearing. Regardless of whom you serve, the only way to get the right attitude is to serve your leader "as working for the Lord," worshiping Him. The attitude of our heart determines whether we act in a spirit of worship or let the flesh reign supreme.

We are called to submit to the authority God places over us. It is always for a reason, painful though it may seem at the time. Keep coming back to this powerful truth; it may well help you overcome immense frustration. It is sometimes not easy, but God's Word will ultimately prevail.

Part of demonstrating excellence is in being really good at what we do. We are to have expertise in what He has called us to. We have stewardship of our talents and a mandate to develop them and use them for God, serving Him in the marketplace. If we know our strengths, then we have a duty to develop them and to unlock our potential. Learning is a lifelong exercise, and we would do well to endeavor to continue developing our talents.

It is popular in human resource circles to take tests that expose our weaknesses and issues that we may have. This is good and very worthwhile. It is through understanding our weaknesses that we can avoid being tripped up by them. However it is in understanding our strengths, and developing them, that we will truly be propelled to our full potential.

The makeup God has given us in our unique set of gifts and natural propensities are only a baseline. It is our duty to grow, nurture, and develop these abilities as stewards of God-given gifts. If we are to fully serve God in excellence, we have an obligation to take our talents and not bury them, but to invest in their development so they may yield abundant fruit for the kingdom.

Perseverance

Why do we always talk about what goes well? We all live in the real world and have experienced failure as well as success. Even in writing this book, I have talked more about the things that went well rather than what didn't go so well.

In our ego-friendly form of Christianity, watered-down to be palatable to our postmodern mindset, we have diluted some of the more-challenging aspects of following Jesus. If we were to truly be like Jesus, our ultimate destiny would be to be ostracized, judged, denied justice, ridiculed, and then crucified.

We don't want to talk about suffering; we don't want to talk about perseverance, patience, and the denying of self. We want all the blessings of God without paying the price. Yes, you are quite correct; Jesus did pay the price. But often if we are to walk the same road He walked and to become like Him, all may not be as easy as we would like it to be. There are times when we experience the dark night of the soul, questioning "why this?" and "why that?" There are many books written on the seven steps to success and not many on how to deal with life when it all goes horribly wrong.

The materialistic consumer mentality that pervades the Western world in particular, coupled with affluence and insulation from true suffering, is not the exclusive domain of the atheist and agnostic. Our Western mindset and worldview permeates the church as much as any other part of society. It is the awareness of the ideology that can help to anaesthetize its effect. If we know we are impacted by a worldview that is not truly Christian, then we must challenge the very way we think and align and test it against the truth revealed to us in the Scriptures.

What we have tended to do is to take the good and leave the bad. He is absolutely the God who gives and takes away. As I said previously, He is more interested in our character than in our prosperity. His agenda is not our agenda. His ways are not our ways. There will always be times when we do not understand what on earth He is doing.

Take for example when He sent Paul to Rome. The Scripture tells us Paul got into the boat, and then we read that the winds were against him. Now if I were God, and thank God I'm not, and I wanted to get Paul to Rome, then he would get the fairest of fair winds and at least a business-class ticket.

Yet in God's dealing with Paul and in His infinite wisdom, not only were the winds against him, but he was also due for a shipwreck, beatings, and even being bitten by a snake. Paul's view of the world seems markedly different from ours.

"Five times I received from the Jews the forty lashes minus one. Three times I was beaten with rods, once I was pelted with stones, three times I was shipwrecked, I spent a night and a day in the open sea, I have been constantly on the move. I have been in danger from rivers, in danger from bandits, in danger from my fellow Jews, in danger from Gentiles; in danger in the city, in danger in the country, in danger at sea; and in danger from false believers. I have labored and toiled and have often gone without sleep; I have known hunger and thirst and have often gone without food; I have been cold and naked. Besides everything else, I face daily the pressure of my concern for all the churches. Who is weak, and I do not feel weak? Who is led into sin, and I do not inwardly burn? If I must boast, I will boast of the things that show my weakness. The God and Father of the Lord Jesus, who is to be praised forever, knows that I am not lying" (2 Cor 11:24–31).

There is a not a lot of comfort in that story other than to know that the will of God will ultimately prevail. The Scriptures are full of stories where God seemingly opposed the very will He had declared. The Israelites roamed around in the desert for over 40 years. When they had finished their meanderings and God's perfect timing to enter the Promised Land had come about, the Jordan was in flood. Of all the times God could have chosen for them to cross over the Jordan, He chose a time when the Jordan was in flood.

Sometimes we can discern what the reason is or apply our simple human logic to what God is doing, but we must remember we are just clay and He is the Potter.

"Yet you, LORD, are our Father. We are the clay, you are the potter; we are all the work of your hand" (Isa 64:8).

The clay does not argue with the Potter, saying, "Why are you making me like this? Shouldn't you be making me like that? Why aren't you doing this? Why are you doing that?"

"But who are you, a human being, to talk back to God? 'Shall what is formed say to the one who formed it, "Why did you make me like this?"' Does not the potter have the right to make out of the same lump of clay some pottery for special purposes and some for common use?" (Rom. 9:20–21).

His ways are definitely not our ways. He is the Master, and we are the servants. Sometimes there will be a hard reality of just not knowing why, and we will feel betrayed by God and let down. This is when we have to choose to believe and operate in faith. It's called faith for a reason. I am not sure I know why, but I get the sense that if we choose to worship and surrender in those times, our faith will go to a whole new level.

Often we are called to take a road less travelled. Sometimes it is tough, and sometimes it is unbearable. But He is with us all the way, whether we feel His presence or not. He will strengthen us to go beyond our human endurance. We will not be tempted or tested beyond what we can bear.

The Israelites were prepared for the battle in 40 years of tough times. They were prepared for obedience and saw the miracles of the hand of God. They had learned to be obedient, and their ranks had been purged of unbelief. The wonderful provision of God was that when the Jordan was in flood, first they needed a miracle to even cross over, but second, when the Jordan is in flood, it is a time of harvest.

Personally, I have seen times of plenty when God opened every door in wonderful ways. He has given me favor and authority and placed me in positions of leadership. He has also taken me through valleys and times of trial.

There have been periods where I have not worked for a season. At one stage, we lost almost everything, and in the midst of that, I began to question God about His faithfulness. I was the clay talking to the Potter. I asked for a word, something to soothe my spirit and to affirm His faithfulness to me, and I expected a promise of restoration. His reply was swift but somewhat lacking in compassion, in my view. I jest now, but then it was a really tough word! It came in the form of a Scripture from the Amplified version.

"If you return [and give up this mistaken tone of distrust and despair] then I will give you again a settled place of quiet and safety and you will be My minister; and if you separate the precious from the vile [cleansing your own heart from unworthy and unwarranted suspicions concerning God's faithfulness] you shall be My mouthpiece" (JER 15:19).

I had some serious adjustments to make in my own heart regarding my view of God. During this time, my populist theology was soundly challenged and shaped. My online ministry, ww.CalledtoBusiness.com, was birthed, and my walk with God was shaken, strengthened, and restored.

Over the next two years, God built us back up financially and spiritually and restored the year the locusts had stolen. That only occurred as I humbled myself, learned the lessons that needed to be learned, adjusted my heart, put away some pride and ego, and chose to trust in a faithful God regardless of what I saw Him doing in my life and regardless of the circumstances.

In the midst of trial, we can worship not only in word and song but also in surrender, obedience, and perseverance. Worship in the midst of trial is precious in God's sight. I am not sure I fully understand the concept or that I really want to find out, but I am convinced of its validity and that in the trials and tribulations of work, we can manifest the act of worship.

Ultimately worship is from the heart. It is a position and attitude of surrender. It is the praise that rises up in good times and bad, regardless of our circumstances. It is evidenced in our work as we not only surrender in obedience but also endeavor to work with excellence, serving Him in the vocation He has purposed for us to fulfill. The very act of working is worship because it is purposed, sanctified, and ordained by God. When we align ourselves to His will and purposes at work, we live and breathe and have our being, in Him.

Key Scripture

"Whatever you do, work at it with all your heart, as working for the Lord, not for human masters" (Col 3:23).

Main Points

- Work is worship.
- Worship is a surrendered heart.
- Obedience heralds the kingdom of God.
- Without humility, there is no worship.
- There is worship in excellence.
- Perseverance in submission is worship.

Prayer

Here I am, Lord, use me. I worship You with all I am and all that I do. Amen.

Notes

CHAPTER 8
WORK IT OUT

"'For I know the plans I have for you,' declares the Lord,
'plans to prosper you and not to harm you, plans to give
you hope and a future'"

(JER 29:11).

Here we are in the concluding chapter of this book. I trust that you have found something in these pages that has been quickened to your spirit and alerted you to the profound understanding that God is vitally interested in you and your workplace.

We have explored the concept that work was God's idea, born before creation itself. If it is His idea, then we should consult Him in how, when, and why we work. If it is His idea, He will have a purpose for our engagement and a method in which to operate. He places us in specific positions to have influence and to work out His plan for our lives. He is intimately aware of us at work, and we need to become aware of Him if we are to be truly effective and fruitful in the workplace.

We have gone on to look at work as a vehicle for provision, which is not a new concept. We have an obligation and duty of stewardship and a need for resources to bless our families, our selves, the broader family of God, and others in need. The vehicle of this provision—work—is often maligned and seen almost as a necessary evil—as if engaging in commerce somehow taints us. Our walk with God is as relevant on Monday while it is being experienced at work as it is in church on Sunday.

We have considered the complex and somewhat contentious way God can use our work life to grow us in character and to help us become more like Him. God places people and circumstances in our lives that cause us to respond. This shapes and molds us as we choose His way rather than ours and as we yield and allow the Holy Spirit to change and influence us. Often these times are tough as we wrestle with our independent will and His Lordship. Yet as we yield and surrender to His program, we will express more of His life. His fruit manifesting in our lives evidences this transformation.

We are now aware of the importance of witness at work, and hopefully you have gained some insight and understanding into how that can occur naturally at your workplace. There is a wonderful opportunity as we rub shoulders and labor with all kinds of people on a daily basis to share who we are and the Jesus we know. This is not an environment where we are to shrink back and endure while waiting to get in a more Christian setting. God will place people around you who need to hear the good news.

Witness is more than telling people about Jesus; it is the demonstration of a transformed life and an empowered one at that. We are called to have an impact at work—to be the ones who restore, heal, and engage. Our work life should reflect our inner life and be a physical manifestation of that transformed life we claim is available. We need to have consistency to have credibility. We can be real, natural, and effective commercially as we are salt and light. There is no inconsistency between being bold in business and being a believer.

We have plumbed greater depths by looking at how we can cooperate in the creativity of God. This unleashes the power of God in our workplaces and moves us beyond our own talents and strengths. God brings growth, favor, and the power of transformation. Through Him we can achieve reconciliation and restoration. He is the God who knows and sees all. By tapping into His purposes, guidance, and power, we are able to achieve so much more. When we align our lives, learn to hear from Him, and begin to do His will, the very kingdom of God is established in our workplace.

We finally moved on to the seemingly ethereal concept of worship and showed how its real definition is based in practical application. We learned that work can be worship when it is done with excellence under the anointing of the Holy Spirit through a surrendered and sanctified heart.

These things are all good ways God can move in the workplace, and I believe the understanding and awareness of these principles will impact your life. But ultimately it is only a revelation of God that will really impart these things to you. They are spiritual in nature and need to be spiritually discerned.

In the chapter on character and growth, I talked about the importance of intimacy. The discipline of taking time out to spend with God has to be a fundamental part of our lives if we want to build intimacy with Him. I cannot emphasize enough the need to walk with Him closely and daily.

While the corporate expression of faith is an important part of the Christian walk and we do need to be part of a living community, ultimately we will stand before God alone. Our effectiveness in the kingdom is born in the times we spend alone with Him, listening, being challenged, learning, and being strengthened and encouraged by our heavenly Father.

Ultimately there is no true business transformation without personal transformation, and it is in our quiet times with God where we really do business with Him. It is our personal walk that is manifest in the public domain. As Proverbs 23:7 says, *"For as he thinks within himself, so is he…"* (NKJV).

It is our hearts that are transformed and ministered to by God. The heart will ultimately drive us, even the words we say, for it is also written in Luke 6:45, *"A good man brings good things out of the good stored up in his heart, and an evil man brings evil things out of the evil stored up in his heart. For the mouth speaks what the heart is full of."*

Those around us will see who we are, good or bad. We need to allow the transforming power of the Holy Spirit to change us into His image so we may be effective and capable for what He has called us to do.

"'For I know the plans I have for you,' declares the Lord, 'plans to prosper you and not to harm you, plans to give you hope and a future'" (JER 29:11).

He has a plan and purpose for our lives, one that includes our work life as much as our personal life and that was written before we were even born. It is a plan that is designed to prosper us and do us good. It is a plan that will help impact the world and one that expands the kingdom of God.

God loves you with a never-ending love. It is a love so great that we cannot begin to understand its depth. He created us lovingly and gave us a purpose and a destiny. We were made perfectly unique, individually crafted to meet His predestined purpose. We can grow to our full, real potential only in relationship with Him. His plans are good, and He has never made a mistake.

The outworking of His creativity, purpose, and plan includes your time at work. Since this is the majority usage of your time, it stands to reason it has an important place in His thinking.

"For you created my inmost being; you knit me together in my mother's womb. I praise you because I am fearfully and wonderfully made; your works are wonderful, I know that full well. My frame was not hidden from you when I was made in the secret place, when I was woven together in the depths of the earth. Your eyes saw my unformed body; all the days ordained for me were written in your book before one of them came to be. How precious to me are your thoughts, God! How vast is the sum of them! Were I to count them, they would outnumber the grains of sand—when I awake, I am still with you" (PSA 139:13–18).

The plan for you is unique and handcrafted by almighty God for you and you alone. No one can have the impact you can have. No one can complete the task that has been assigned for you. God is more interested in seeing His will done then you are. All we need to do is to be available and obedient. He has anointed and appointed you for a purpose. That, as I am sure you have gathered by now, is the key to understanding how God works at work.

There are a few simple things you need to do and a couple of principles that are important to unlocking your full potential at work. This potential is only realized as you are in Him. Therefore the glory is all His.

Pray

Take the things you have learned in this book, and talk with Him about them. He is very resilient and patient, and He already knows what you are thinking. Take the time to build a true relationship with God. It will become your most precious time. If you already do this, then why not talk more about work? You may be surprised by what He has in mind. You can always go deeper.

Renew

Renew your commitment to Him, and choose to surrender again to His will and purposes. Surrender once more to the all-powerful One who created you and everything you can see. He wants your heart; yield it to Him and enjoy the wonderful sense of peace that pervades those intimate times. If you struggle to hand things over to Him, be willing to be willing, and He will take you the rest of the way.

Invite

Ask Him to come in and impact your workplace. He can be a gentleman, and He has chosen to wait to be asked. Call on Him to intrude in all that you do at work. Bring the business, situations, and people at work before Him, and invite Him to come in.

Commit

Take a short period of time each day to read His Word and spend time with Him. Set aside some time, and make it a priority to spend time with your Father. These simple disciplines will revolutionize your life. As you study His Word, ask the Holy Spirit to give you understanding and to enlighten you to the application in your life.

Expect

Look for His hand at your work. You have invited Him in, and He will be working in and through your workplace. Watch for the opportunities and the ideas that begin to flow. Act on the impulses, and expect to hear Him at work.

These seemingly simple things are paying the P-R-I-C-E—an understated anagram to remember the disciplines of walking with Him. Why not even do those things now, before other things distract you? Please bear in mind that you are in a battle, and you have a number of weapons and strategies that have been placed before you to use in establishing God's kingdom at work.

This book is meant to draw you closer to God and challenge you to invite Him into your workplace. It has hopefully answered the question of how to integrate your faith into your workplace. I trust God has impacted you as you have prayerfully considered these things. I am still on the same journey of understanding what it means to be a minister in the marketplace and to be called to business.

It is only fit and proper that I leave the last word to Him. The Scripture below encapsulates what it is to be God's person in the workplace. It covers our responsibilities at work, how we should act, and the importance of what we are doing.

Thank you for taking the time to read this book. I trust it has been a blessing to you. God bless you as you seek to serve Him in your workplace.

"Servants, respectfully obey your earthly masters but always with an eye to obeying the real master, Christ. Don't just do what you have to do to get by, but work heartily, as Christ's servants doing what God wants you to do. And work with a smile on your face, always keeping in mind that no matter who happens to be giving the orders, you're really serving God. Good work will get you good pay from the Master, regardless of whether you are slave or free. Masters, it's the same with you. No abuse, please, and no threats. You and your servants are both under the same Master in heaven. He makes no distinction between you and them. And that about wraps it up. God is strong, and He wants you strong. So take everything the Master has set out for you, well-made weapons of the best materials. And put them to use so you will be able to stand up to everything the Devil throws your way. This

is no afternoon athletic contest that we'll walk away from and forget about in a couple of hours. This is for keeps, a life-or-death fight to the finish against the Devil and all his angels. Be prepared. You're up against far more than you can handle on your own. Take all the help you can get, every weapon God has issued, so that when it's all over but the shouting you'll still be on your feet. Truth, righteousness, peace, faith, and salvation are more than words. Learn how to apply them. You'll need them throughout your life. God's Word is an indispensable weapon. In the same way, prayer is essential in this ongoing warfare. Pray hard and long. Pray for your brothers and sisters. Keep your eyes open. Keep each other's Spirits up so that no one falls behind or drops out" (EPH 6:5–18 MSG).

EPILOGUE:
A WORD TO
CHURCH LEADERS

First, thank you for reading my book. If you have endured my somewhat incoherent ramblings up to this point, I trust you have received this in the spirit with which it was written. If you have jumped to this page, I encourage you to take the time to read the rest of this book. The businesspeople under your care will appreciate your understanding of these principles.

I hold leaders of churches in high esteem. You have the inevitable task of shepherding the people of God. It is often a thankless task with a lot of responsibility before God, and I have seen the price that has been paid by some.

I have had the privilege of being in a number of different denominations. God has taken me to many different fields. Some were conservative, and others would be considered extreme by some. In all these congregations, in many different locations, from Catholic to Baptist, from Presbyterian to Pentecostal, I have seen and met men and women committed to God. Many have been business leaders of all shapes, sizes, and persuasions; the vast majority of them comfortable working full-time.

I'm committed to the local church. It is in this expression of God's kingdom that we enjoy the corporate solidarity of community. The weekly expression of worship and teaching is an important part of my life. It is within this context that this book is written.

Many who profess to be in marketplace ministry have put aside the local church out of a sense of frustration. This frustration has come from a lack of understanding of the calling the majority have to minister in their workplace. Many church leaders are threatened by the concept of the laity ministering of their own accord outside the realms of the organized church. However, I believe it is in the encouragement of this ministry and the releasing the full potential of the church to go out once more into the highways and byways that will advance the kingdom of God.

It is in the understanding of the broader picture where the kingdom of God takes priority over the local church and the growing of a local institution, where we will truly impact the world for Christ. We cannot control the kingdom of God, so we are reliant on trusting the Holy Spirit to orchestrate its expansion and impact as He sees fit. Sometimes what is considered chaos is actually the freedom of allowing Him to be effective.

I had the privilege and pain of helping plant a church in South Auckland. It gave me an insight into the challenges of church planting, church leadership, and church growth, so I have some limited insight, and a lot of sympathy, for the challenges you have as a church leader. It was in this capacity that I first realized I was equating a person's spirituality and commitment to God with the amount of spare time he or she was giving up to build the church. My worldview was segmented.

Church leaders are, quite rightly, preoccupied with the growth, or at least the health, of the local church over which they preside. This is not unreasonable; in fact, it shows a healthy sense of responsibility. The downside is that this is entirely centered on activities involving the organized church: prayer meetings, ministry meetings, church meetings, officially sanctioned church events etc. In church, we pray for the Sunday school teacher with her twenty students, whom she has for two hours on a Sunday, and forget that she impacts over one hundred kids for the kingdom of God during her forty-hour working week.

For the vast majority of working people, there is a significant sacrifice of family and recreational time, given with the best intentions, to engage in church activities. My contention is that if there was an understanding of the calling of God for each of us in our workplace, with no separation between secular and sacred, then we would all be impacting the world twenty hours a day.

Imagine a congregation released into their callings, effectively reaching the lost, and impacting their communities for Christ. Your church would be so full you wouldn't have capacity to control it even if you wanted to. Then the church leadership would truly be fulfilling the Ephesians mandate.

"So Christ himself gave the apostles, the prophets, the evangelists, the pastors and teachers, to equip his people for works of service, so that the body of Christ may be built up until we all reach unity in the faith and in the knowledge of the Son of God and become mature, attaining to the whole measure of the fullness of Christ. Then we will no longer be infants, tossed back and forth by the waves, and blown here and there by every wind of teaching and by the cunning and craftiness of people in their deceitful scheming. Instead, speaking the truth in love, we will grow to become in every respect the mature body of him who is the head, that is, Christ. From him the whole body, joined and held together by every supporting ligament, grows and builds itself up in love, as each part does its work. For it is the people who need to do the work, and that will build up the church" (Eph 4:11–17).

APPENDIX: Jobs in the Bible

Ambassador	2 CORINTHIANS. 5:20
Archer	GENESIS 21:20
Armor-bearer	JUDGES 9:54
Athlete	2 TIMOTHY 2:5
Baker	GENESIS 40:1
Banker	MATTHEW 25:27
Blacksmith	1 SAMUEL 13:19
Bodyguard	1 SAMUEL 28:2
Bowmen	ISAIAH 21:17
Brickmaker	GENESIS 11:3
Builder	2 KINGS 12:11
Butcher	MATTHEW 22:4
Carpenter	MARK 6:3
Charioteer	1 CHRONICLES 19:18
Cook	1 SAMUEL 8:13
Counselor	2 SAMUEL 15:12
Courier	2 CHRONICLES 30:6
Creditor	DEUTERONOMY 15:2
Cupbearer	GENESIS 40:1
Designer	EXODUS 35:35
Doorkeeper	2 KINGS 22:4
Embroiderer	EXODUS 35:35
Emperor	ACTS 25:25
Engraver	EXODUS 28:11
Executioner	MARK 6:27
Farmer	2 TIMOTHY 2:6
Fisherman	ISAIAH 19:8
Gardener	JOHN 20:15
Gatekeeper	2 SAMUEL 18:26
Gem cutter	EXODUS 28:11
Goldsmith	ISAIAH 40:19
Governor	2 KINGS 23:8
Grape picker	JEREMIAH 49:9
Grinder	ECCLESIASTES 12:3

Guard	1 Samuel 22:17
Harpist	Revelation 14:2
Harvester	James 5:4
Herdsmen	Genesis 13:7
Horseman	2 Kings 9:17
Hunter	Genesis 10:9
Innkeeper	Luke 10:35
Instructor	Proverbs 5:13
Interpreter	Genesis 42:23
Jailer	Acts 16:23
Judge	Exodus 2:14
Keeper of flocks	Genesis 4:2
King	Genesis 14:1
Landowner	Matthew 20:1
Lawyer	Acts 24:1
Magistrate	Luke 12:58
Maidservant	Deuteronomy 15:17
Manservant	Exodus 20:10
Mason	2 Kings 12:12
Merchant	Matthew 13:45
Messenger	1 Samuel 23:27
Metal forger	Genesis 4:22
Midwife	Genesis 35:17
Minister	Isaiah 61:6
Moneylender	Exodus 22:25
Musician	Psalms 68:25
Oarsmen	Ezekiel 27:8
Officer	1 Chronicles 26:24
Overseer	Acts 20:28
Perfumer	1 Samuel 8:13
Philosopher	Acts 17:18
Physician	Jeremiah 8:22
Planter	Amos 9:13
Plowman	Amos 9:13
Poet	Acts 17:28
Potter	Isaiah 29:16

Preacher	2 PETER 2:5
Priest	GENESIS 14:18
Proconsul	ACTS 13:7
Prophet	GENESIS 20:7
Queen	1 KINGS 10:1
Rabbi	MATTHEW 23:7
Reaper	2 KINGS 4:18
Refiner	MALACHI 3:3
Robber	JOHN 10:1
Satrap	EZRA 8:36
Scribe	1 CHRONICLES 24:6
Seer	1 SAMUEL 9:9
Servant	GENESIS 15:3
Shepherd	1 SAMUEL 21:7
Silversmith	JUDGES 17:4
Soldier	JOHN 19:23
Spy	NUMBERS 21:32
Steward	GENESIS 43:16
Stonecutter	2 KINGS 12:12
Stonemason	2 SAMUEL 5:11
Swordsman	2 KINGS 3:26
Tax collector	MATTHEW 10:3
Teacher	1 CHRONICLES 25:8
Tentmaker	ACTS 18:3
Treasurer	EZRA 1:8
Trumpeter	2 KINGS 11:14
Vine grower	JOEL 1:11
Warrior	JUDGES 11:1
Watchman	2 SAMUEL 13:34
Water carrier	JOSHUA 9:21
Weaver	EXODUS 35:35
Woodcutter	JOSHUA 9:21
Woodsman	2 CHRONICLES 2:10
Writer	PSALMS 45:1

About the Author

Mark Bilton BSc, DipBus, MBA

Mark has extensive experience working as a CEO, director, and managing director in private, multinational, and publicly listed companies. His specialty is creating value through strategy, vision, and culture, and he describes himself as a "change catalyst." His most recent position was as the CEO of Hagemeyer Brands Australia, which was transformed and divested on behalf of listed multinational French owners Rexel in less than two years.

Mark was recently appointed to the Gloria Jean's Coffees board, helping to oversee one thousand coffee houses in over thirty countries. Mark has held numerous commercial and not-for-profit directorships on industry, charitable trust, leadership, international missions, and educational bodies.

Mark recently was presented the Terry Plochman Award for being the world's best YPO Forum Officer in front of over two thousand CEOs in Denver by the premier leadership body the Young Presidents Organization.

He has a passion for business and for Christians in the marketplace. His online ministry, Called to Business (www. CalledtoBusiness.com), uses social media to "encourage and equip Christian business leaders to be effective in the marketplace." Mark has a master's in business administration, a post-graduate diploma in business, and a bachelor's of science.

He has been married to Helen for twenty years, has three young children, and lives in Sydney.

Bibliography

John C. Maxwell. 2007. *The 21 Irrefutable Laws of Leadership: Follow Them and People Will Follow You.* Thomas Nelson.

John C. Maxwell. 2011. *The 360 Degree Leader: Developing Your Influence from Anywhere in the Organization.* Thomas Nelson.

Michael R. Baer. 2006. *Business as Mission: The Power of Business in the Kingdom of God.* YWAM Publishing.

David McCracken. 2011. *An Incorruptible Heart: Having Influence without Losing Your Integrity.* David McCracken Ministries.

Mark Greene. 2010. *The Great Divide.* The London Institute for Contemporary Christianity.

Ed Silvoso. 2009. *Anointed for Business: How to Use Your Influence in the Marketplace to Change the World.* Regal.

Larry Burkett. 2006. *Business by the Book: Complete Guide of Biblical Principles for the Workplace.* Thomas Nelson.

Rich Marshall 2000. *God@Work.* Destiny Image Publishers.

Os Hillman. 2010 *Faith at Work Movement: What Every Pastor and Church Leader Should Know.* Aslan Group Publishing.

Recommended Resources

Called to Business: www.CalledtoBusiness.com

Monday Matters author Mark Bilton's online ministry to "Encourage and equip Christians to be effective in the workplace".

You will find many resources including a powerful weekly biblical business e-Message that you can receive in your email.

You can find Called to Business on the social media sites listed below:

www.Facebook.com/CalledtoBusiness
www.Twitter.com/Calledto
www.YouTube.com/CalledtoBusiness

Monday Matters: www.MondayMatters.net

The home of Monday Matters books and resources.

You can find Monday Matters on the following social media sites:

www.Facebook.com/MondayMatters
www.Twitter.com/MondayMatters

Mark Bilton: www.MarkBilton.com

Monday Matters author Mark Bilton's personal blog.

You can find Mark Bilton on the social media sites listed below:

www.Facebook.com/MarkBilton
www.Twitter.com/MarkBilton
www.Linkedin/in/MarkBilton
www.YouTube.com/MarkBilton
www.Pinterest.com/MarkBilton

Other Recommended Marketplace Ministries

www.**MarketplaceLeaders**.org

Os Hillman is president of Marketplace Leaders, an organization whose purpose is to help men and women discover and fulfill God's complete purposes through their work and to view their work as ministry. Marketplace Leaders exists to help men and women fulfill God's call on their lives by providing a FREE devotional that goes out to over a quarter of a million people all over the world and by training business leaders to see their work as a catalyst for change through training events and other ministry events.

www.**LICC.org**.uk

LICC exists to envision and equip Christians and their churches for whole-life missionary discipleship in the world. They seek to serve them with biblical frameworks, practical resources, training and models so that they flourish as followers of Jesus and grow as whole-life disciple making communities. Mark Greene is one of the most articulate and effective communicators in the marketplace today.

www.**GodatWork**.org.uk

In his book God at Work, Ken Costa writes about how the Christian faith should and can be lived out in day-to-day life at work.

As a high profile banker in the City of London, he considers the challenges of living out his faith at work and speaks openly of his own struggles with ambition, money, relationships, success and failure.

By using the Biblical principles that underpin his faith and applying them to the 21st century workplace of today he offers practical advice on tackling the common problems familiar to many: the work-life balance, stress, ambition, failure and disappointment.

www.**BusinessasMissionNetwork**.com

The most comprehensive source of information about the Business as Mission Movement with many links to numerous companies, resources and articles.

www.**EdSilvoso**.com

One of the most effective Marketplace Ministers in the world, transforming many businesses and lives as he teaches comprehensively in many countries.

www.**JohnMaxwell**.com

Still one of the best and most respected experts and teachers on leadership and personal growth.

MON**D**AY
memos

A daily devotional for those in the workplace.

By Mark Bilton

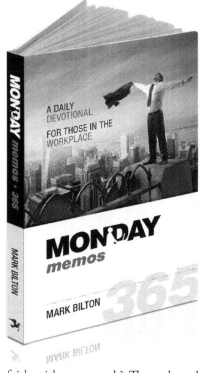

Does God really have a plan and a purpose for my work?

God is vitally, passionately, and intimately interested in the workplace. Many have embraced the biblical concept of our whole life being impacted by God, and that there is no separation between the sacred and the secular.

How do you integrate your faith with your work? Through real commercial experience, author Mark Bilton has walked with God and seen Him open doors that have taken him from the shop floor to the boardroom; from sales assistant to CEO.

In this book are 365 short, sharp, insightful messages that are scriptural and applicable to you and your work. They will transform your work life, and your workplace. There is no inconsistency between a Christian worldview and commercial success.

Work is a vital part of His plan and purpose for us. We have been lovingly crafted, anointed and appointed, for a particular purpose. We will only reach our full potential as we recognise God's hand at work in our work.

www.**MondayMemos**.com